The Small Biz Quickstart Workbook

The Ultimate Guide for First Time Entrepreneurs

Karl W. Palachuk

Published by

Great Little Book Publishing Co., Inc.
Sacramento, CA

www.GreatLittleBook.com

This page left intentionally blank.

(Well, obviously, that didn't work out as planned.)

Great Little Book Publishing Co., Inc.
Sacramento, CA

The Small Biz Quickstart Workbook: The Ultimate Guide for First Time Entrepreneurs, by Karl W. Palachuk.

ISBN 978-1-942115-57-1   (Paper)
ISBN 978-1-942115-58-8   (PDF)
Library of Congress Control Number 2020906441

Production Notes: Cover design by Sally Galli. Layout by Yvonne Betancourt. Other graphics by Kara Schoonveld. All mistakes by Karl W. Palachuk. Primary fonts are Minion Pro Medium and Lucida Console.

www.greatlittlebook.com

This page left intentionally blank.

(This is clearly not working, so we won't do it anymore.)

The Small Biz Quickstart Workbook

The Ultimate Guide for First Time Entrepreneurs

Karl W. Palachuk

Table of Contents

Your Downloadable Content

This workbook includes additional downloads that you will find very helpful.

If you purchased this product from SMB Books or Great Little Book, you should have received a download link when your purchase was completed. If you have problems finding this, email concierge@smallbizthoughts.com.

If you lost that or purchased from Amazon or another reseller, you can register this book at **SmallBizQuickstart.com.**

Note on Used products: We have to assume that the first owner of a product registered it and downloaded the bonus material. Therefore, we do not supply downloads to people who bought this product used. Thank you for understanding.

Your feedback is always welcome.

So, You Want to Be Self Employed

Congratulations on taking the plunge! As scary as it seems right now, quitting your job to start your own business will be one of the highlights of your life. A few notes of caution are in order.

First, please be very sure that you are *willing* to take the plunge. I know it's a good decision, and I've never met you. But *you* need to know it's a good decision. You need to be completely committed so you will move forward and not look backward.

I've always said that bad managers have created more entrepreneurs than any other force in nature. **Everyone wants to quit their job sometime. But when you want to quit your job *all the time*, then you don't have any choice.**

Second, is your family ready for you to take the plunge? You will probably have to work longer hours in the beginning. And you may take a cut in take-home pay for quite some time.

But most importantly, you will fall in love with your new job. Your family will enjoy many benefits from your new freedom, but they need to be prepared for you to spend a certain amount of emotional energy in a relationship with your work.

Third, you need to make sure you are the kind of person who will be successful as an entrepreneur. That means you are self-motivating, you can work effectively alone, and you are good at organizing your work.

If you're unsure, that's okay. One of the benefits of this workbook is to help you learn about what it takes to start and run your new business.

The Three Categories – And Timing

The workbook is divided into three categories: Planning, The Launch, and The First Year. These are the major stages of launching your business.

The Planning tasks are designed to help you think through all the little details before you make the plunge. The really good news here is that you can take as long as you want to go through them.

But please don't sit on the fence for years. The fact that you're holding this book in your hands means that your unconscious, emotional brain has already made the decision to start a business. Now you need to work through the rational details so that you can justify your decision (to yourself and others).

Whether you think of it in these terms or not, the primary motivator for *not* starting your business is fear. Fear is fed by a lack of knowledge. In this case, almost all fear is fear of the unknown. When you start your next business, you won't have fear about anything in the Planning stage of this workbook. Really.

Depending on where you are in the mental journey to starting your business, you may go through the Planning tasks very quickly or very slowly. The faster you go, the more likely it is that your unconscious brain has already decided to make the jump.

Sort the Tasks

Here's my advice on using these tasks. First, browse through them all and pick out the ones you've already finished. For example, if you already have a domain name or an office to work out of, then you can check the **Completed** box and move on. (Also, pat yourself on the back.)

Second, sort the remaining tasks. I recommend sorting them from highest to lowest priority. You get to decide the priority. Start by labeling them **High, Medium,** and **Low.**

You may also sort them based on how difficult you think they are. And you get to decide whether you want to tackle the difficult or easy tasks first.

Another option is to sort them into the order you think you'll execute them. Some of them have to be executed in order (for example, you have to have a tax ID before you can open a bank account in the business name). Most of them, however, you can decide the order.

As you can see, there is some suggested order, but it's ultimately up to you. I hope that you will enjoy jumping in and swimming in this project.

The Launch tasks are for the period when you actually execute the departure from your job and the creation of your business. These are actions that you need to take immediately before and after the moment you quit your job. With luck, and this book, this period should last no more than one month.

There are lots of tasks related to getting your finances in order (insurance, bank accounts, etc.). Many of these are easy to do and should be done before you make the plunge. Overall, you need to feel that you've built enough of a safety net so that you feel comfortable giving your notice.

As with the Planning tasks, you need to sort through the Launch tasks and mark those you've already completed. Then sort the remaining tasks and begin executing.

When you have finished the Launch tasks, you will have executed everything you need to get ready for the move, quit your job, and get your business going. It really will be very, very cool!

The Year One tasks are all the little things you need to think about going forward. Most of them are basic tasks that help you run your business, like invoicing and making tax payments. Some are longer term and you will repeat them again and again.

Again, you'll sort the Year One tasks, mark those you've already completed, and then sort the remaining tasks as you see fit.

Full Time, Part Time, Or What?
(Professional, Semi-Pro, Or Amateur?)

Many people make the mistake of believing you can start a business part-time in your basement. One in a hundred thousand business owners make that work. (I just made that up, but I'm pretty sure it's true.)

If you keep your job and start your business on the side, you will literally break your own heart. You will work hard all day for "the man" you hate, then work six or eight additional hours trying to build your business.

But you'll be giving your tired, worn-out self to your new company. And you'll be trying to do it after hours when you can't return phone calls, prospect for new business, and even begin to understand how good your new business could be.

Alternatively, you could work on your business during weekends. You'll have more energy and do a better job, but you're basically in the same situation.

Oh, and did you have a family somewhere along the way? Do they get any of your time?

Obviously, I am very biased. I believe that you should make a clean cut when the time comes. Do the Planning work! Go through the Launch work. Embrace it. Love it. Bring 100% of your energy to your new job – and be a professional!

If you haven't read Steven Pressfield's *Turning Pro* or *The War of Art*, take time to read them. In the end, you are either a professional or an amateur. Decide.

Make Good Habits and Become Their Slave

Much of life, as well as your business, depends on your developing good habits. And really, not just good. Good habits will make you good at your business. Great habits will make you great.

One of my favorite lines is from Og Mandino's book *The Greatest Salesman in the World*: "I will form good habits and become their slave." The reason this is true is that we are all ruled by our habits. But we get to choose the habits we form.

As you begin operating your business, you should constantly evaluate the habits you have and the habits you need. For example, I hate calling people and making sales. Hate. Hate-hate-hate. I hate it so much that I refuse to do it.

So, I've built an entire business process that does not require me to ever call someone on the phone and ask them for money. I'm so dedicated to this process that I've built a half-million dollar business that requires zero outbound sales.

To achieve that, I've had to be rigorous about the habits of marketing, blogging, social media, and newsletter writing that create a massive in-bound marketing machine.

Business is like that a lot. If you don't like a specific activity, or you refuse to do it, then you need to figure out alternatives that help you achieve the same result as those activities.

And when it comes to all the basic tasks of running a business, there's a long list of things you need to be good at. Most of them are not difficult at all – like invoicing on time, writing press releases, and paying the rent. They just need to be done.

Those are perfect examples of habits you need to learn to execute consistently and flawlessly. This is not a matter of skill or ability – it is purely a matter of habit.

As a coach, I help many companies figure out why they're stuck and how they can get to the next level. In every single case, over more than ten years, the client knows exactly what their problem is and what they need to do to fix it.

It always boils down to this: They have bad habits; they need good habits. And the reason everyone knows that we're talking about habits is that it's 100% about behavior. The problem is rarely about strategy. It's always about execution.

Make the formation of habits your work and your success is guaranteed.

Be Supremely Honest with Yourself

Human beings have an optimism bias. If we didn't, we'd never have children. But most of us are predisposed to believe that good things will happen to us and bad things won't.

You can't fool yourself in business. You have to be honest with yourself about your level of commitment, your self-discipline, your skills, your abilities, and your knowledge.

If you're not committed, you need to accept that. If you are unsure about whether this is right for you, be honest. If you are paralyzed by fear, accept that.

All of those things can change. But if you are not committed, not sure, and feeling more fear than excitement, you need to go work on those things. All of them are reversible. You can address your fears and short-comings.

When you work on this project long enough, all that hesitation will disappear. At some point, you'll be so excited about opening your business that nothing will stand in your way.

Starting your business is a lot like getting married. If there's a doubt, it's best to stop and go address that before you proceed.

When you believe that you have all the skills, ability, and ambition, then it's time to start working full-time on your new business.

Growing from One to Two, Three, and Ten

At some point you're going to need help. That might mean outsourced contracts and services. Or it might eventually mean hiring employees.

Here are a few things to consider about employees:

It is best to start with a part-timer, for several reasons. Full-time employees are very expensive. And I would recommend that you have enough profit or "spare" money in your business to cover an employee's salary, plus expenses, before you hire.

A safe calculation is salary times 1.25. If you provide benefits, the cost will go up from there. You need to pay Social Security taxes of about six percent of salary. Plus worker's comp, unemployment insurance, etc.

With a part-time employee, you can easily adjust hours when your cash flow changes. And don't feel guilty about hiring people part-time. There are lots of people who only want to work 10-20 hours per week.

College students and stay-at-home parents are the best. They are educated and sincerely only want to work limited hours.

When it's time to hire someone full-time, please make sure that you have the cash flow to keep them. It is very sad and emotionally draining to have to lay off an employee because you didn't have the money you thought you had!

Hiring your first employee is literally the greatest percentage growth your business will ever experience.

The very good news is that your new employee will double the number of hours available in your business. Maybe you will use those hours to sell services, or complete lots of administrative work. Whatever your new employee does, you will be able to expand your capacity.

I recommend that you hire an administrative assistant as your first employee. You will be tempted to hire someone to do your technical or primary work. That labor will probably be much more expensive than an administrative assistant. And an admin will free up your time to either perform the primary labor or make more sales.

YOU Are Probably the Actual "Product"

Among the big decisions you have to make are the name of your company and your overall brand. Over the years, I have owned several companies, including KPEnterprises Business Consulting, Inc., Relax Focus Succeed, and Great Little Book Publishing Co., Inc.

Within those companies I have had many products, services, and web sites. But I learned a very important lesson with three very different audiences: In the end, *I* was the brand. You may have the same experience.

In my service business, my clients always felt that they had a direct relationship with me – even when I had twelve employees. And when I developed online services and communities, I discovered once again that no one paid attention to the various brands I used. Again, I was the brand.

If you do a good job of creating your brand by being an interesting and engaging marketer, then people will know you – and they may not know your various brands separate from you.

One way to know whether you are the brand is to look at your web statistics from time to time. Among the juicy details you'll find there are the search terms people entered in order to find your site.

If people are searching for "Your Company" or "Your Brand," then that's a great indicator that your company is your brand. But if people are searching for "Your Name Company" or "Your Name Brand," then people are really searching for your name. And that makes you the brand.

Why does that matter?

Once you determine whether your brand is you or your product, you can use that information in your future marketing and branding. If your brand turns out to be you, then you need to start using that.

That's all good when it comes to marketing right now, today.

You also need to look way down the road to your exit strategy. That is, how will you get out of this business? Will you sell it? Take on investors? Sell controlling interest and stay involved for a year? Or maybe pass the business to your children.

If you intend to sell your business someday, or even pass it along to your children, you will need to separate your company branding from yourself as an individual. You may not need to make any changes now. Just be aware of it when you start working on your exit strategy.

You Don't Have to Get It Perfect the First Time

Many people are stymied by the mistaken belief that they have to "get it right" before they implement decisions. This includes small decisions as well as large ones.

I encourage you to take a different approach: Accept that this is an iterative process. That means you will tackle the same decisions again and again. Eventually, you will get good at making decisions. The sooner you give up believing in perfection, the sooner you can learn to make decisions quickly, without fear of being wrong.

Consider your business five or ten years from now. You will have run many marketing campaigns. With each one, you will learn something about what works and what doesn't. And, ideally, each campaign will be better than the previous.

The same is true with your price lists, your offerings, your strategies, and everything else in your business. Everything changes, all the time. It is simply impossible for you to keep doing exactly the same thing all the time.

So, you see, every decision you make in preparing for your business, launching your business, and executing the first year will be revisited at some point.

So just remember that you need to go through this process, but execution is far more important than getting it right the first time.

The Japanese have a management process called Kaizen. It means constant, incremental improvement. Embrace that philosophy and relax; you have forever to get it right!

Is Your Family Ready for You to Be Self-Employed?

If you have a family, you need to consider whether they are ready for you to make the launch into self-employment. It's great that you are excited and have faith in your future. But a new business can be very difficult on a family.

Many new business owners un-balance their lives terribly. They believe they need to take every customer who walks in the door. They tend to work very long hours, leaving almost no time for their family.

This behavior compounds until something blows up. And that something is often the most important relationship in your life.

Take this very seriously. It's important to talk about the long hours, and the struggles ahead, and all the things you're not sure about. When a partner knows what they're getting into, it is much easier for them to support you when the going gets tough.

It's also a good idea to set some limits on your work time. You need to have balance in your life if you're going to make this business work in the long run. You need to spend time relaxing and recharging your batteries.

And remember: The more you talk about all these things with your partner, the smoother everything will go – the first year and every year after.

Work-Life Balance

One of my first books is called *Relax Focus Succeed*. It's all about balancing your personal and professional lives and being more successful in both.

This balance is always a challenge. Everything in your life and business changes all the time. So you need to keep working on balance forever.

What does that mean? Ideally, it means that you consciously create your business – and re-create your life – so they are completely in synch. You need time to work, time to play, time with your family, time to work on your personal self, and time to recharge your batteries.

I know all that sounds like an impossible balance, but it is very manageable if you plan it out and work to make it happen. It might take years to achieve a sustainable, healthy balance, but it absolutely is possible.

Stress and exhaustion really do kill people. Build sustainable habits and you will be able to practice them forever.

It may seem impossible to imagine now, but you can create a balance between personal time, family time, and work time that allow you to have the best of all worlds. Most people never achieve this balance for one simple reason: They never try.

Creating work-life balance takes a great deal of time, attention, and work. If you start your business with the intention of creating this balance, and fine-tuning it forever, then you can create a successful balance that improves every part of your life and work.

Think of Yourself Separate from Your Business

No matter what happens in your business, you need to think about yourself separate from your business. You are you, playing a role inside your business. You need to always maintain this distinction between yourself and your business.

Here's why this matters. At every stage of your business, your business has a character and a personality. It has specific financial requirements. It has needs and it generates rewards. All of these things change over time.

In the meantime, you have a changing role within your company. You might become an employer or an outsourcer. You might take on a partner, buy another company to merge with, or sell your business to another company.

No one who's been in business for five years will tell you that they foresaw every single thing that happened in their business.

When I started my first business, I just wanted to make some money from my knowledge of computers and politics. Within one month of starting my business, I had dropped the political consulting and become a technology consultant.

A year later I was deep into consulting within an industry I'd never heard of when I started. Five years after that I had a few employees and had started moving down the road that would lead to my second corporation, my first book, and a business completely unrelated to what I started out doing.

Your business will grow and morph over time. As it changes, you will need different things from your business. You will probably start out wanting money from your business. Over time, it will probably become a source of creative inspiration. And, if you're lucky, your clients and associates will become among your closest friends.

Eventually, you may decide to change the form of your business (for example, from a sole proprietorship to corporation). Or you might change your focus from one industry to another. There are many changes you might make.

At every stage, you will do well to think of yourself as the owner of the business – not as the business itself. In the hard times, you will need to make hard decisions and push the business to pay your full due. When you deal with employees, partners, clients, and associates, you always need to be the owner.

If you lose sight of this and see yourself as the business (and the business as your self), you will end up making bad financial decisions. For example, if the business is losing money, you might lose clarity of thought as you do whatever it takes to keep your business alive.

As extreme as that seems, it is very common. Remember: 80% of all businesses fail. And very often that failure is a result of confusing our personal ego with the business itself.

Even if you have to get rid of all your employees and go back to a business of one person, this is better than going out of business because you made bad decisions that led to borrowing money, growing debts, and potentially filing for bankruptcy.

I know this sounds extreme. But mark your calendar and re-read this chapter one year from today. I promise it will make a lot more sense!

Make Your Finances Your Absolute Highest Priority

I have owned one or more businesses since 1995. I have been coaching business owners for more than fifteen years. So, I've seen lots of businesses, lots of plans, and lots of "profit and loss" reports.

Even after all that, I was surprised at how many topics in this workbook fall under the topic of finances. Over the years, I have learned that I have to take care of state and local taxes, licenses, employee expenses, supplier accounts, etc., etc., etc.

I only point this out because it really struck me how much I wish I'd known when I quit my job and jumped into a business!

As a result of listing all the things you need to take care of – over 100, it turns out – I was surprised that 25% of them addressed some form of finances. And if you throw insurance-related tasks on the same pile, you're at about 40%.

The lesson is clear: If you want to take your business seriously, you need to take your finances seriously! And if that means taking some classes or reading some books, you need to do that.

There are certain financial topics you need to take extremely seriously, and never take chances with. The top three, as far as I'm concerned, are taxes, employees, and cash flow. Rather than restating advice here, I simply encourage you to take very seriously the advice on those three topics: taxes, employees, and cash flow.

Accountants, Enrolled Agents, And Tax Professionals

There are lots of references here to accountants, enrolled agents, and tax professionals. Please take this as a sign that you need to rely on these folks for advice.

I have found that a great tax professional is one of the best resources your company will ever have. Personally, I prefer an enrolled agent who can represent me before the IRS, if necessary. It has never been necessary – in large part because I use an enrolled agent to prepare my taxes.

But wait: That's not all!

Tax professionals are also great business advisers on many levels. They see many more businesses than yours. They see businesses of all kinds, with a wide variety of opportunities and challenges.

And most importantly, these folks understand the tax implications of the actions you take. Should you hire someone part-time or use a contractor? There are tax implications. Should you rent an office? The tax implications depend on how your business is formed.

Time and time again, you will find that business decisions affect your taxes in ways you probably did not foresee.

See the chapter entitled "The Paradox of Simplicity." Please don't do a mediocre job on your taxes when a tax pro will always do a better job.

Introduction to Recurring Revenue

If there's one thing that comes close to magic in business, it's recurring revenue.

If you make a one-time sale of $1,000, you get to put $1,000 in the bank. But if you make a recurring sale of $1,000, you get to put $12,000 in the bank every year.

Not every business can create recurring revenue, but if you can figure out a way to do it, I encourage you to do so. It is worthwhile to get creative here. As you look through your credit card statements, you will find many subscriptions. These might include a monthly dog box mailing, a car wash service, lawn care, or many other services.

Your recurring revenue offering might be a product or a service. It might be billed monthly or annually. No matter what it is or how you invoice for it, this offering can do wonders for your business.

Recurring revenue grows until it becomes a solid floor under your feet. This is "guaranteed" revenue every month. With luck, it will grow to cover your core expenses and your payroll. After that, it will grow to give you a steady profit on top of everything else.

All that sounds good. But recurring revenue does something else as well. It gives you freedom. It allows you to take some chances and try new things, safe in the knowledge that the rent will be paid and the employees will be paid.

In other words, it gives you the freedom to constantly breathe new life into your business.

Late Charges, Finance Charges, And Treating Your Business Like A Business

One of the most common mistakes made by new business owners is to extend credit to clients and not charge them extra for paying late and treating you like the bank. I made this mistake. In fact, most of the business owners I know have made it.

If you make this mistake, you will go down a road to some difficult lessons. Clients will pay you late – because there's no penalty for late payment and, therefore, there's no reason to pay on time. You will also have difficult conversations with clients if you start to enforce rules you haven't enforced before.

I recommend that you adopt the following policies, no matter what your business:

1) Get paid in advance for everything. This is true for both products and services.

2) If you allow clients to make payments for anything (ignoring rule one), you should charge late fees and interest when clients pay late.

If you don't set and enforce these policies, you *will* eventually learn the hard lesson that there are people who simply don't pay their bills on time – and a few who never pay at all. As you have one bad experience after another, you will begin to adopt rules to keep bad things from happening again.

The first hard lesson is that money owed to you is never paid in full. And the more this debt grows, the less likely it is that you'll be paid at all. This is no joke: I've had someone tell me that they can't ask a client for the $70,000 they're owed . . . because "They're my best client." All I could think of is, Who's your worst client?

When debt grows like that, you eventually have to have a difficult conversation. Two things will come out of that. First, you will accept less than the full payment just to get rid of the debt. Second, you will lose this client. Either you will drop them or they will drop you.

Good riddance, I say.

The most I ever lost was a couple thousand dollars – which hurt a lot at the time. But it taught me to put rules in place to keep this from happening again.

Here's the very odd part about putting the policy in place to get paid in advance for everything: There's never any push-back. I have coached thousands of business owners to do this. Some had been allowing clients to owe them money for years.

And ninety-nine percent of every one who ever instituted this policy and reported back to me was surprised that no one batted an eye. Paying for things before you take delivery is a basic, non-controversial policy. Just do it.

If you wish to help your clients make payments, there may be several options available to you. Depending on your industry, your suppliers, and the manufacturers you work with, you may be able to point them to various programs to finance the products and services you provide.

There are all kinds of financing options, including leases, that are designed specifically to help businesses buy things and make payments over time. Find them and introduce your clients to them.

The Paradox of Simplicity

We live in an era of great technology. It becomes smarter, more capable, and easier to use all the time. But there's a downside to that: Each of us can do an "okay" job of someone else's job.

I call this the Paradox of Simplicity. If I have little or no skills with graphics, for example, the tools can never make me great. But they allow me to do a mediocre job. That's the simplicity.

The paradox is that so many people can now do a half-baked job of so many things that they avoid paying to have those things done the right way by professionals.

You need to be aware of both sides of this paradox. If you can honestly do a good-to-great job by yourself, then consider doing it. But if you can only do a mediocre job, please hire someone to do it right. That might be an employee or a contractor.

At the same time, you need to understand that many potential clients will not hire you if they think they can do the job themselves. This will be a constant challenge in your business. Don't be irritated or frustrated by this. It is simply a fact. But DO be aware that this challenge is out there, and try to figure out how you can fight it.

One of my favorite examples of the Paradox of Simplicity is taxes. I can't tell you how many business owners I've met who still do their own taxes, rely on the software, and end up paying tens of thousands of dollars extra in taxes. When it comes to relying on professionals, start with a tax pro.

Relax. No Decisions Are Permanent.

Many of the tasks in this workbook represent topics you will visit again and again. And sometimes you might be surprised at the decisions that you revisit.

For example, you might decide to change the name of your company, or the way it's legally formed. You might take on new products, or focus on different clients.

Some plans will only last a year or two. Others might last ten. But here's the important point: Do not stress out about anything in this workbook.

If you get the wrong business model, you'll figure it out and find the right one. If your logo sucks, or your bank charges too many fees, you can find a better one.

Spend time talking to enough business owners and you'll learn about every mistake you can imagine – and a few you can't. It's amazing how many bad turns your business can take and come out stronger in the end.

Critical mistakes – the kind that kill businesses – almost never happen at once. They generally involve letting your cash flow get out of hand, going into debt, and gradually digging a hole you can't get out of. And that's not one mistake. It's a series of mistakes. Or a broken process that never got fixed.

So, forge on. Full speed ahead. Every decision needs to be made, and you should make the best decision you can, but don't freak out and don't worry about making mistakes.

Stage One: Planning

PLANNING: MARKETING

Chutzpah

Chutzpah (pronounced hut-spa) is a Yiddish word for audacity, nerve, or supreme self-confidence.

Do you have the chutzpah it takes to quit your job, create a business, and fight the odds? Statistically, the odds are against you! Do you have what it takes to go from a "known" income to zero dollars per month?

On the face of this, it sounds like a bad bet. But talk to any entrepreneur who is five or ten years into self-reliance, and they will all tell you that they wish they had left their job earlier!

If you decide that you do not have what it takes, STOP NOW. You can spend ten or twenty years chasing a dream with half your heart and half the commitment you need. If your really don't have what it takes, that's okay. Spend your life making money at a job and don't' worry about the one-in-a-hundred chance of making a living as an entrepreneur.

Complete! _____

Priority: H   M   L

Due Date: _____

Assigned To: _____

Resources Needed: _____

_____

_____

_____

Notes: _____

_____

_____

_____

_____

_____

_____

PLANNING: CLIENTS

Getting Your First Clients

How will you find your first client? What do they look like?

Define your ideal client. How big are they? What projects do they bring to you?

You might think it sounds silly, but you need to create a model client profile. That means you need to define a "perfect" client, and figure out how you will sell to that client. Is your model client a male or female? How old? Married or single? And so forth.

You might create two model clients: One male and one female; or one twenty-something and one forty-something. Define who you will sell to, and define every detail you can think of.

Once you have a very clear focus on your model clients, then you can go and find them. What are their challenges, dreams, and opportunities? And most importantly, why will these clients do business with you? What do you offer that they can't get anywhere else?

Complete! _____

Priority: H   M   L

Due Date: _____

Assigned To: _____

Resources Needed: _____

_____

_____

_____

Notes: _____

_____

_____

_____

_____

_____

_____

PLANNING: CLIENTS

How Do You Get Customers?

Every business needs a few key methods for acquiring new clients. You might offer a free report, pay for referrals, or develop another process.

You may start with a preferred method or two. You should be open to trying new things as your business evolves. If something works well, add it to your favorites.

If your clients are local, join local networking groups or the Chamber of Commerce, hold lunch and learn events, or speak to local meetup meetings. If your clients are remote (national or international), then you'll need to use social media, online marketing, and related services to get clients.

Assignment: Spend a month listening to the commercials you normally ignore. What methods are these folks using to get new clients? Are these methods appealing to you as a buyer? How about as a seller.

Decide: How will *you* get new customers in your business?

Always rely on a small number of successful proven methods to grow your business. This is a resource unique to your business. Nurture it and rely on it again and again through the years ahead.

Complete! _____

Priority: H   M   L

Due Date: _____

Assigned To: _____

Resources Needed: _____

_____

_____

Notes: _____

_____

_____

_____

_____

_____

_____

PLANNING: CLIENTS

Pick A Niche or Two, or Three

It seems counter-intuitive to many people that you should focus your business on a niche market. People often say, "I want to sell to everyone: It's a larger market." But you can't sell to everyone. And marketing to everyone is the same as marketing to no one.

When you focus your attention on a smaller market, you can become an expert within that field. Think about meeting a doctor (or lawyer, or farmer, or roofer) at a cocktail party. How long will it take for this person to know that you do not understand their profession? The answer is about two minutes of conversation.

Why? Because you do not use their terminology. Even if you know some terminology, you don't use it quite right. But if you spend years working with a specific profession, you will learn their challenges, their opportunities, and their terminology. You will become a special kind of insider who can offer them services that other "generalists" cannot.

Complete! _____

Priority: H   M   L

Due Date: _____

Assigned To: _____

Resources Needed: _____

_____

_____

_____

Notes: _____

_____

_____

_____

_____

_____

_____

PLANNING: FINANCES / TAXES, ETC.

Be Prepared to Make Tax Payments

When you are self-employed, you need to pay your taxes directly to the state and federal governments (assuming your state has an income tax). If you are a sole proprietor (using your personal social security number as your tax ID), your business expenses show up in a specific schedule on your tax return.

If you are a corporation, LLC, or some other entity, you will file a tax return for the corporation and then the profit or loss will flow to your personal tax return. See your tax preparer or enrolled agent for all the details!

In most cases, you will need to make quarterly estimated tax payments. There are federal and state forms for this. You pay your money to the IRS (the Treasury). You need to keep track of it because you need to enter these estimated payments into your tax return. The important lesson here is, you need to take care of this in a timely manner! Don't forget about it. Set the money aside and don't spend it on anything else.

What will you do to prepare for this?

Complete! _____

Priority: H   M   L

Due Date: _____

Assigned To: _____

Resources Needed: _____

_____

_____

Notes: _____

_____

_____

_____

_____

_____

PLANNING: EMPLOYEES

How Many Employees and When?

Things change over time, and you need to be open to that. But, when it comes to employees, you need to start with a plan for your first few years in business. Do you need employees? If so, how many?

Depending on your business, you may be able to grow for years before hiring your first employee.

Many new business owners worry about employees for years before they decide to take someone on. You can avoid this waste of mental resources by deciding well in advance that you won't start making plans to hire someone until your reach a certain point.

You can always revisit this decision. But it helps to start with a direction to take for the first year or so.

Complete! _____

Priority: H   M   L

Due Date: _____

Assigned To: _____

Resources Needed: _____

_____

_____

_____

Notes: _____

_____

_____

_____

_____

_____

_____

_____

PLANNING: EMPLOYEES

Planning for Growth: Slow Versus Fast

You might be surprised, five or ten years from now, how many times you get asked the question about how fast you want to grow. The answer affects whether vendors want to partner with you and whether banks or investors want to lend you money.

Pay no attention to what others think a business like yours should do. If you are happy with a specific pace of growth, that is all that matters. Fast or slow, this decision will influence many others.

If you want to grow quickly, you need to put significant resources into a sales machine. You will also look at large funding sources from private equity, corporate stockholders, or even a public offering.

If you want to grow slowly, you need to focus very clearly on cash flow and set clear targets for how you will expand – either one client at a time or one employee at a time. What is your strategy?

As always, no decision is irreversible. But making a decision will help you head in the direction you wish to go.

Complete! _____

Priority: H   M   L

Due Date: _____

Assigned To: _____

Resources Needed: _____

_____

_____

_____

Notes: _____

_____

_____

_____

_____

_____

_____

_____

PLANNING: EMPLOYEES

Who Is Your First Hire?

Many business owners are tempted to hire clones of themselves as their first hire. This happens, generally, because the workload grows and you need a "technician" to complete the work.

Consider, instead, an administrative assistant, bookkeeper, or office manager who can relieve a great deal of your workload at a fraction of the cost. I encourage you to take this seriously and consider which of your regular chores could be passed on to someone else.

Divide your duties into three piles: High, Medium, and Low technical skills required. Pass off those that require the fewest technical skills – or require skills you don't have or jobs you don't enjoy. Believe it or not, there are people who love all the things you find boring or tedious!

There are many people willing to take on administrative duties part-time. This includes college students and stay-at-home parents who have great skills, but only want to work in the middle of the day while their kids are in school.

Complete! _____

Priority: H   M   L

Due Date: _____

Assigned To: _____

Resources Needed: _____

_____

_____

_____

Notes: _____

_____

_____

_____

_____

_____

_____

_____

PLANNING: FINANCES

Basic Monthly Financial Reports

Early on you should determine the metrics you will use to evaluate the performance of your business every month. This may include the number of sales, the number of clients, and other measures of success. It will also include costs for key components of your business.

These monthly financial reports are different from a simple "Profit and Loss" report (see the task on P&L). These reports will focus on leading indicators such as appointments set and lagging indicators such as sales closed.

You will have to determine what you want to measure every month. These reports are very personal to your business. You will have to determine over time what success looks like inside your company.

Action Step: Analyze your future business. Spend some time considering how you will measure success.

Complete! _____

Priority: H   M   L

Due Date: _____

Assigned To: _____

Resources Needed: _____

_____

_____

_____

Notes: _____

_____

_____

_____

_____

_____

_____

_____

PLANNING: FINANCES

Billing: Invoicing and Cash Flow

Cash is the oxygen of business. Managing cash flow is critical. One of the most important tasks you need to perform is invoicing. You must invoice consistently. That might mean immediately upon a sale, weekly, or monthly. Whatever you decide, never let this slip.

And no matter how much you want to resist it, you should charge late fees and charge interest on past-due invoices. You are not the bank. And it is always harder to add these charges after letting clients slip for months than it is to enforce these policies from the beginning.

Better yet, you should try to get prepaid for everything you do. Or, start a project with a fifty percent down payment and an agreed upon payment schedule after that. Many people wish they had taken this excellent advice when they started their business instead of ten years later.

Complete! _____

Priority: H   M   L

Due Date: _____

Assigned To: _____

Resources Needed: _____

_____

_____

_____

Notes: _____

_____

_____

_____

_____

_____

_____

_____

PLANNING: FINANCES

Cash Flow Projection - Year One

If you've never owned a business, you may have never dealt with cash flow before. A cash flow report is just what it sounds like: A look at the amount of cash you have on hand over a certain period of time.

Think of it like a check register with a balance column. Invoices and bills are not entered here. Cash flow is only affected by the actual cash coming into or going out of your bank account. Someone might owe you $50,000, for example. The bank considers that an asset. And with luck you'll see that money someday. But on the day your electric bill is due, available cash is all that matters.

Cash flow boils your financial status to three simple entries: Money in, money out, and total available. For example, which payments do you actually expect to hit your bank account by the next pay period? And which bills must be paid? If your information is accurate, you'll know whether or not you have the money needed for payroll.

You should create a rough cash flow report by month for your first year. Unlike a business plan, you are encouraged to update this frequently. With experience, your projections will become more accurate as time passes.

Download: Register this book at www.smallbizquickstart.com to get a sample cash flow projection.

Complete! _____

Priority: H   M   L

Due Date: _____

Assigned To: _____

Resources Needed: _____

_____

_____

Notes: _____

_____

_____

_____

_____

_____

_____

PLANNING: FINANCES

Create Your Chart of Accounts

A chart of accounts is the name bookkeepers and accountants give to all the line items in your finances. This includes the primary categories of Revenue and Expenses. Within each of these, you will find a line for each income or expense category.

Assuming you use QuickBooks, or something similar, your financial program will help you set up your chart of accounts. It is very helpful to engage an accountant or enrolled agent to make sure your chart of accounts is set up properly from the beginning.

After your business is up and running, you will need to generate reports for your accountant as well as various state and federal government agencies. And of course, you'll need to run a properly formatted Profit and Loss report when it's time to file your taxes.

Action step: Find a good tax professional to help you set up your Chart of Accounts.

Download: Register this book at www.smallbizquickstart.com to get a sample chart of accounts.

Complete! _____

Priority: H   M   L

Due Date: _____

Assigned To: _____

Resources Needed: _____

_____

_____

_____

Notes: _____

_____

_____

_____

_____

_____

_____

_____

PLANNING: FINANCES

Prep Last Three Years Tax Returns

Before you quit your job, you should make sure you have three years' worth of tax returns available when someone asks for them. Ideally, this will be in PDF format and not something you have to photocopy.

If you need to clean up old issues in your taxes, do the best you can. And do it as soon as you can.

This will become far less important as time goes on. Once you have a year or two of earnings, you can point to actual performance rather than your previous financial status.

Depending on how you plan to finance the first few years of business, you may not need these tax returns. But if you wait, it will be more difficult to clean up as time passes.

Complete! _____

Priority: H   M   L

Due Date: _____

Assigned To: _____

Resources Needed: _____

_____

_____

_____

Notes: _____

_____

_____

_____

_____

_____

_____

_____

PLANNING: FINANCES

Profit & Loss - Forecast Years 1-2-3

Your projected first-year profit and loss (P&L) report is handy for many reasons. First, you should create it for your own uses. You need to have a good understanding of your income and expenses going forward.

If you look for financing from a bank, or investors of any kind, they will want to see your forecast. Even some vendors and distributors will request it.

Once you have a first-year projection, you should go ahead and estimate income and expenses for years two and three. As you make these projections, you should also make notes about *why* income and expenses will go up or down. You cannot simply increase revenue 10% per year for no reason!

Over time, you will revisit this forecast many times. You should always have an idea of how money flows into and out of your company. As with many other things, your forecasts should grow more accurate over time.

Download: Register this book at www.smallbizquickstart.com to get a starter spreadsheet for your first P&L.

Complete! _____

Priority: H   M   L

Due Date: _____

Assigned To: _____

Resources Needed: _____

_____

_____

Notes: _____

_____

_____

_____

_____

_____

PLANNING: FINANCES

Funding: What Do You Need To Start?

How much will it cost to open your business? Do you need furniture, office space, computer equipment, or other major expenses? Will you be able to use your cell phone as a primary business phone, or will you need a phone system of some kind?

Services you might need include web site development and hosting, accounting, legal, marketing, and insurance. Finally, consider what you will need in license fees, permits, and incorporation costs.

You should be able to get some estimate of each of these. Keep this on a tracking spreadsheet and replace estimates with actual numbers when you have them.

Complete! _____

Priority: H   M   L

Due Date: _____

Assigned To: _____

Resources Needed: _____

_____

_____

_____

Notes: _____

_____

_____

_____

_____

_____

_____

PLANNING: FINANCES / TAXES, ETC

How Will You Pay Federal and State Taxes?

As discussed in a different chapter, you will need to make estimated tax payments.

Under certain circumstances, you may also be able to make some or all tax payments through your company payroll. If you are a sole proprietor, this is normally not an option. But if you have employees and run payroll through a service, you will be able to pay yourself a paycheck and pay tax payments through normal deductions.

If you pay yourself through payroll, you may wish to limit your pay to a specific amount in order to save money on taxes. Talk to your tax adviser. And track everything you do!

Just be aware that limiting your payroll will not reduce your overall tax bill. In other words, if you pay yourself $1,000 less but make an extra $1,000 profit, you'll still have to pay taxes on that money. As a result, you will probably need to make estimated tax payments, even if you pay most of your taxes through payroll.

Complete! _____

Priority: H   M   L

Due Date: _____

Assigned To: _____

Resources Needed: _____

_____

_____

_____

Notes: _____

_____

_____

_____

_____

_____

_____

Cap Ex vs. Op Ex Spending

A capital expenditure (capex) is an expense for acquiring physical assets, such as computer or manufacturing equipment. As a rule, cap ex purchases become assets on your balance sheet and are depreciated over time.

Operating expenditures (opex) are expenses that appear on your profit and loss report as an expense and do not show up on the balance sheet as an asset. Opex includes things like rent and marketing.

In some cases you can choose whether to "expense" something in a specific year and choose to consider it opex rather than capex. Each of these affects your tax calculations, so get advice from a professional. One of the arguments in favor of cloud services is that your can reduce capex by buying hosted services, which are opex.

Complete! _____

Priority: H   M   L

Due Date: _____

Assigned To: _____

Resources Needed: _____

_____

_____

Notes: _____

_____

_____

_____

_____

_____

_____

PLANNING: FINANCES

Home Office Deduction

This topic never seems to stop changing. Can you take a home office deduction? That depends on a lot of things. The rules change from time to time, so always check with your tax adviser!

Generally speaking, if you have someplace else to go to work (e.g., an office), then you cannot take the home office deduction. If you have nowhere else to go, then you can take some kind of deduction.

Depending on your circumstances, the deduction may be based on the percentage of square footage of your house dedicated to your office. This may also be affected if you are a renter versus a home owner. And rules are different for sole proprietors and corporations.

Do your research and figure out what you plan to do.

Complete! _____

Priority: H   M   L

Due Date: _____

Assigned To: _____

Resources Needed: _____

_____

_____

_____

Notes: _____

_____

_____

_____

_____

_____

_____

_____

PLANNING: STRATEGY

Build vs. Buy Your Business

Should you build your own business, or buy an existing one? And if you buy one, should it be a franchise?

The advantage of buying a business is that they have an existing client base and known income stream. In addition, a well-run franchise will have a proven business model that is constantly improved.

The disadvantage of an existing business is that they have processes and procedures that you consider broken, and you will need to fix these over time while continuing to run the business. An existing business may also have clients and vendors you do not want. Again, you will need to make changes over time.

Either approach can be successful. Plan carefully.

Complete! _____

Priority: H   M   L

Due Date: _____

Assigned To: _____

Resources Needed: _____

_____

_____

_____

Notes: _____

_____

_____

_____

_____

_____

_____

_____

PLANNING: FINANCES

Automobile Expenses

If you use your car for work, you can generally take a mileage deduction to cover expenses. There are a few rules (for example, your first and last trip of the day are your commute and not deductible), but it's generally straight forward.

If you have employees, you might reimburse on the same schedule, or provide employees with a stipend to use their cars for work purposes.

One other option, down the road, is to have a car that is completely dedicated to work and is either owned or leased by the business. Obviously, this is the most expensive option and has the most rules you need to follow. You probably don't want to start with this option. Just be aware of it.

Complete! _____

Priority: H   M   L

Due Date: _____

Assigned To: _____

Resources Needed: _____

_____

_____

_____

Notes: _____

_____

_____

_____

_____

_____

_____

PLANNING: FINANCES

Consider Staying Home

Many people assume that a "real" business has to have a real office. I highly encourage you to wait as long as possible to give up your home office in favor of an outside option. Even if you cannot take a home office deduction, renting office space is almost guaranteed to be more expensive.

Once you open an office, related expenses will grow very quickly. Whether you planned it or not, you will end up buying furniture, kitchen supplies, networking equipment, and more. Even if you need very little in the way of office supplies, you will end up buying more once there's a shelf to put them on.

Another consideration is having employees show up at your home. Depending on your circumstances, this may the point at which a home-based office is more trouble than it's worth.

Complete! _____

Priority: H   M   L

Due Date: _____

Assigned To: _____

Resources Needed: _____

_____

_____

_____

Notes: _____

_____

_____

_____

_____

_____

_____

_____

PLANNING: INSURANCE

COBRA Health Insurance

COBRA – the Consolidated Omnibus Reconciliation Act – allows you to stay on your employer's health insurance plan, even if you quit or are fired. You have to pay the full price for this insurance, and possibly a small administrative fee.

You can stay on a COBRA plan for up to eighteen months. This gives you significant time to find a new group policy or individual coverage.

Your employer's insurance plan should be able to give you more information and let you know what your options are. Be sure to shop around. COBRA may be an expensive option compared to buying insurance directly.

Complete! _____

Priority: H   M   L

Due Date: _____

Assigned To: _____

Resources Needed: _____

_____

_____

_____

Notes: _____

_____

_____

_____

_____

_____

_____

_____

Binding Arbitration

You may wish to include a clause in your contracts to invoke arbitration rather than allowing disputes go to court.

One place to start is the American Arbitration Association at https://www.adr.org.

That web site includes "clauses" you can use in your service contracts as well as a list of arbiters in case you need one.

It's much easier to get a client to agree to arbitration in your contract than it is in the middle of a dispute. So it's good to make this decision before you Launch your business.

Complete! _____

Priority: H   M   L

Due Date: _____

Assigned To: _____

Resources Needed: _____

_____

_____

_____

Notes: _____

_____

_____

_____

_____

_____

_____

_____

PLANNING: LEGAL

Contracts and Terms of Service

You should absolutely have some kind of contract with your clients. The contract will define your terms of service and guide the relationship. Remember, when everything's going great, no one will read the contract. But when things go bad, both sides will read it. Make sure you have a good one.

The "statement of work" is not part of the contract. It is guided by the contract. But the contract (also called a service agreement) is not about the service you provide; it's about the relationship.

The greatest advantage of a contract is that it defines your client relationship in the eyes of the government and the courts. Are you an employee or a contractor? That's defined, in large part, by your contract.

If you can find a sample contract for your industry online, that's great. But remember two things: 1) "Free" is normally the most expensive option; and 2) Absolutely have a lawyer review your contract to verify that it does what you want, and it's enforceable.

Complete! _____

Priority: H   M   L

Due Date: _____

Assigned To: _____

Resources Needed: _____

_____

_____

_____

Notes: _____

_____

_____

_____

_____

_____

_____

PLANNING: LEGAL

Find an Attorney

You will need an attorney to review your service agreement(s). If you need something more than a basic service agreement, you should write your own agreement, specific to your business. Then have it reviewed by an attorney.

A good attorney will always review your contract, and make sure it's consistent with state law. If they write something from scratch, the cost will be much higher, and the resulting contract will be more generic.

At times you may also engage attorneys for advice on employee matters, intellectual property, and other matters. Yes, they cost money. But in the long run, they should save more than they cost.

Complete! _____

Priority: H   M   L

Due Date: _____

Assigned To: _____

Resources Needed: _____

_____

_____

_____

Notes: _____

_____

_____

_____

_____

_____

_____

PLANNING: LEGAL

Patents, Trademarks, Service Marks

Do you have, or plan to develop, intellectual property (IP)? If so, you should create some kind of tracking system to make sure you know what you own, the form it takes, how it is used, and how it is protected (copyright, registered trademark, service mark, etc.).

If you own IP before you start your business, you have to decide whether you will use it inside your business. Whether yes or no, you need to document your ownership. If you use your IP inside your business, will the business pay you a licensing fee or royalty? Write out a "memo of understanding" between yourself and your business.

Finally, as you develop IP within your company, you need to decide who owns it: You personally or your company? As someone who has written many books, developed lots of software, and produced a number of proprietary processes, I have always kept ownership of IP to myself personally.

Remember: Intellectual property can be licensed a million times, but it can only be sold once!

Complete! _____

Priority: H   M   L

Due Date: _____

Assigned To: _____

Resources Needed: _____

_____

_____

_____

Notes: _____

_____

_____

_____

_____

_____

_____

_____

PLANNING: MARKETING

Brain Storm. How Do You Reach Your Target?

This is an exercise you should complete with friends or advisers you trust.

First, you need to determine what your target is. Perhaps it's $250,000 in revenue, or $250,000 in profit. Perhaps it's a certain number of superstar clients, or to reach a certain level of notoriety within your profession.

Second, consider every option that might bring you to your goal. It might include creating certain products, using social media, starting a new coaching program, developing software, or many other options.

This kind of soul-searching should be done as often as you can manage – for the rest of your business life. If you do not have a mastermind group, find one or create one. If you don't know what that is, look it up.

Complete! _____

Priority: H   M   L

Due Date: _____

Assigned To: _____

Resources Needed: _____

_____

_____

_____

Notes: _____

_____

_____

_____

_____

_____

_____

_____

PLANNING: Marketing

Branding / Logo / Artwork

Branding is more than your logo: It is every single thing you do in your business.

But for now, let's focus on the most basic elements of branding. Your logo, artwork, and "look and feel" should be modern and professional. But please don't get carried away putting lots of time and money into this. You can always change your logo and visible branding.

Very often, new business owners put lots of energy and time into this kind of thing. Five, ten, and fifteen years later, they start a new project by spending $250 for a design contest and let their employees decide which is best. In other words: Be professional, but don't spend an inordinate amount of time or money on this project.

Complete! _____

Priority:　H　　M　　L

Due Date: _____

Assigned To: _____

Resources Needed: _____

_____

_____

_____

Notes: _____

_____

_____

_____

_____

_____

_____

PLANNING: MARKETING

Web Site Design and Build

Obviously, you need a web site. Unless you are going into the web site design business, PLEASE make absolutely no attempt to design and build your own web site. This is true even if you are super creative, and even if you are super technical.

Web sites can be expensive and complicated. And, yes, you may be ripped off. So it's good to proceed carefully, have a very good idea of what you want, and talk to several designers. In addition to looking at designs, interview each designer and ask why they are using the technology they recommend. After each interview, ask each designer why they recommend a different technology.

Set your budget for web site development so that it hurts a little, but not too much. At least for your first web site, the goal is to look professional – not provide a massive, interactive, database-driven monstrosity that costs thousands of dollars per year to maintain.

Complete! _____

Priority: H   M   L

Due Date: _____

Assigned To: _____

Resources Needed: _____

_____

_____

_____

Notes: _____

_____

_____

_____

_____

_____

_____

PLANNING: MARKETING

Brochures. NO.

This is just a reality check. Think back to every tri-fold brochure you have ever held in your hands. Did you read it front to back? Did you read every single word? And most importantly: Did you make a decision and spend thousands of dollars because of a brochure you read?

My guess is, NO! If you read a brochure and decided to spend a fortune or change your life, I hope you kept that brochure. I'd love to see it.

Here's my point: Of all the money you could spend on advertising, videos, printing, etc., please do not spend one penny on brochures. If you do them yourself, they will be amateurish. If you have them produced professionally, they will cost you a fortune.

Next: Wait ten years. If you're still in business, consider whether you want to spend money on printed brochures.

Complete! _____

Priority: H   M   L

Due Date: _____

Assigned To: _____

Resources Needed: _____

_____

_____

_____

Notes: _____

_____

_____

_____

_____

_____

_____

PLANNING: STRATEGY

Mission / Vision / Values

Many people scoff at the whole concept of creating documents to spell out your company's mission, vision, and values. At the same time, you can find thousands of books, videos, and training materials on this subject. At some point you have to admit that there's value in this stuff.

I believe you should spend lots of time – over a long period of time – discerning which values are central to your personal and professional lives. Please see my book *Relax Focus Succeed* for a deep dive into the personal piece of your journey.

Spend time deciding what's important in your life, and what will be important in your business. Consider (for a very long time): Why does your business exist? Why are you doing this? Simply hating your boss or hating your corporate life is not enough.

In large corporations, your job exists to fulfill the needs of the organization. In small business, your company exists to fulfill your personal dreams and ambitions. That's serious stuff! Are you starting a business to fund your retirement, get your kids through college, buy a second home, fund a charity, fulfill a creative desire? Or something else?

Complete! _____

Priority: H   M   L

Due Date: _____

Assigned To: _____

Resources Needed: _____

_____

_____

Notes: _____

_____

_____

_____

_____

_____

_____

PLANNING: STRATEGY

Name Your Company

I've written several blog posts about this. It's important that you think about a name that will stand the test of time. If you choose a name that's cutesy, humorous, or childish, be sure that's a conscious choice. You can always change your company name, but you'll take a (small) public relations hit as a result.

You may need two names: One for the company itself (the corporation, LLC, or legal entiry) and the name you do business under (DBA = "Doing Business As"). Your corporate identity will have a tax ID number, will execute all legal agreements, and will be the name on bank accounts and other official relationships. Your DBA will represent your company to your clients. You might have more than one DBA.

Overall, your name (at least your DBA name) should be professional and represent your company well among the clientele you choose. Your name may be a good choice, especially if you do not plan to grow into a large company. You "and Associates" is often a good choice. Bottom line: Think about it and make good choices that will last for the next five years.

Complete! _____

Priority: H   M   L

Due Date: _____

Assigned To: _____

Resources Needed: _____

_____

_____

Notes: _____

_____

_____

_____

_____

_____

_____

PLANNING: STRATEGY

Take A Personal Assessment of Your Skills

Consider which skills you'll need to be successful. Are you good at marketing? Finances? Delegating to others?

As you look through these tasks, and all the tasks you'll need to execute before, during, and after your launch, look for skills you'll need. In particular, look for skills that you don't have. You'll need a lot of financial acumen, for example. If you don't have it, how will you get it?

Make a list of all the skills you think you'll need. You obviously have some core "technical" skills in your chosen industry. But focus on all the other skills you might need: inventory, documentation, managing outsourced labor, hiring, firing, negotiating, selling, and so forth. This might be a very long list.

Finally, rate yourself. Use either a 3-point or a 5-point scale. There needs to be a Great, a Poor, and a Middle. Some things you will learn through experience. Others will require education. How will you acquire this? It might be via books, audio programs, classes, online training, or something else. Build your self-education plan.

Complete! _____

Priority: H   M   L

Due Date: _____

Assigned To: _____

Resources Needed: _____

_____

_____

Notes: _____

_____

_____

_____

_____

_____

_____

PLANNING: STRATEGY

What Kind of A Business Plan Do You Need?

Elsewhere we address the finances you'll need, as well as your clients, your vision, and your products and services. We've also addressed how large you want your company to be, how many employees you want to have, and how you want to get there.

Your business plan could be two paragraphs, one page, ten pages, or fifty pages, depending on your answers to all these other questions. The bottom line is: Why do you need a business plan?

Do you need a business plan to guide yourself through the next year? Do you need it to find investment partners? To convince a bank to give you money? Whatever you decide, you will write a business plan specifically for the goals you have set for yourself.

This is a chore you will revisit again and again. You might even consider a "public" and a "private" business plan. The private can be one simple paragraph you revise every year. It will cover your long-term plans. A larger public document for public consumption may address the goals for the next year of the immediate future.

Note: I have a handy dandy Kindle Book entitled *Business Plan in a Month* for only 99¢. Check it out. Just go to Amazon and search for Palachuk *Business Plan in a Month*.

Complete! _____

Priority: H   M   L

Due Date: _____

Assigned To: _____

Resources Needed: _____

_____

_____

Notes: _____

_____

_____

_____

_____

_____

PLANNING: STRATEGY

What's Your Exit Strategy?

I know it seems odd to think about getting out of this business when you're about to get into it. But you should at least speculate about your options. Will you sell it for a chunk of change that allows you to retire? Will you merge with a partner and then step down in the new business? Will you hand the business over to a child, a partner, or a business associate?

There are many options. But consider two things. First, your business will have value over time, so please don't just walk away and close the doors. Second, the end games you have available to you will mold the way your run your business.

For example, if you plan to sell the business, you should run it to maximize profit. If you plan to pass it to a child, you may run it to minimize taxes. Whatever you decide to do, you will optimize your company to achieve one set of goals in operation and another at the "end game."

Complete! _____

Priority: H   M   L

Due Date: _____

Assigned To: _____

Resources Needed: _____

_____

_____

Notes: _____

_____

_____

_____

_____

_____

PLANNING: STRATEGY

Will You Start Part-time or Full Time?

Some people have the option of dedicating one day a week to their new business, and then two days, three days, etc. If your business is to be successful in the long run, you will eventually work at it full time. How long will this transition take?

You may commit to full time in the new business because you quit your job (got fired, retired, etc.). Or you may work up to it a little at a time. Whichever you choose, you should have a plan. How do you get from "Launch" to full-time?

Along your journey – whatever it looks like – you'll need to focus on your finances a great deal. How do you support yourself at each step of the way?

Complete! _____

Priority: H   M   L

Due Date: _____

Assigned To: _____

Resources Needed: _____

_____

_____

_____

Notes: _____

_____

_____

_____

_____

_____

_____

PLANNING: STRATEGY

Be Careful of Bundles When Buying

Bundles are amazing – when you're selling. When you're buying, you need to be a little more careful. Do not buy a bundle of services from one source if it ties you into one provider and you end up paying more in the long run for a core component of the bundle.

For example, your business bank will try to tie you into a line of credit, a business checking account, and merchant services (credit cards) all in one bundle. If you resist on one of these, the bank will change the terms on the others. They will do whatever it takes to tie you into a collection of services that will give them the most money in the long run.

At times (for example, early on in your business) it will make sense to take advantage of these bundles. But in the long run, you will do better by maximizing the profitability of each item individually.

Add this to your list of topics you need to revisit once a year.

Complete! _____

Priority: H   M   L

Due Date: _____

Assigned To: _____

Resources Needed: _____

_____

_____

_____

Notes: _____

_____

_____

_____

_____

_____

_____

_____

PLANNING: PRODUCTS AND SERVICES

The Magic Of Three-Tiered Pricing

You'll have to spend a lot of time figuring out your pricing, no matter what your business is. Two bits of advice about pricing: 1) Ignore your competition. Whatever they're doing or charging is irrelevant to your business. 2) No decisions are irreversible. Whatever pricing you come up with, there is no chance you will have the same pricing model five years from now.

Having said all that, I encourage you to consider selling bundles of products or services. One of the most common offerings you'll see is the three-tiered price list. Used strategically, such a price list can make you a great deal of money. How do you use a price list strategically?

Many people are tempted to create three distinct levels of value. And you can make some money that way. Here's a better approach. Create a basic-level tier and a top level tier (let's call them silver and platinum). Finally, create a tier that offers almost everything in the top tier, but with an important component missing. Then make the price just slightly cheaper than the top tier.

Thus your gold tier is designed so that clients are tempted, but choose platinum instead. If you plan it right, you will never sell a gold package. A few will buy silver and the vast majority will buy platinum.

Complete! _____

Priority: H   M   L

Due Date: _____

Assigned To: _____

Resources Needed: _____

_____

_____

Notes: _____

_____

_____

_____

_____

_____

_____

PLANNING: PRODUCTS AND SERVICES

What Do You Sell and What Do You Charge For It?

I'm sure you have some idea about what you'll sell – both goods and services. Write down a list. Eventually, you'll start speculating about what you'll charge. But start with the list.

You can get ideas based on what others are selling. Just be aware that all such research puts you into an existing marketplace. The best you can do by following someone else is to be second place. But selling into this market will go a long way toward introducing you to the buyers, sellers, vendors, and suppliers in that market.

Whether you create a unique offering sooner or later, you will need to create one if you want to create a new market with no competition. The ultimate business is one where clients come looking for you. Do you want to be *an option*, or the only option?

Complete! _____

Priority: H   M   L

Due Date: _____

Assigned To: _____

Resources Needed: _____

_____

_____

_____

Notes: _____

_____

_____

_____

_____

_____

_____

PLANNING: PRODUCTS AND SERVICES

Set Your Hourly Rates

You don't really have to finalize your rates until you launch. But you should have an idea so you can begin creating a budget.

Here's a truth that too many people learn too late: You will probably never bill 1,000 hours in a year. And you will rarely even reach that number. So please do not budget as if you will sell a "full time" equivalent of 2,000 hours per year.

Based on 800 or 900 hours maximum, how much money do you need to make?

Note also that there's even more money to be made with flat fee pricing. Anything you can do to move away from trading dollars for hours is a move in the right direction.

Complete! _____

Priority: H   M   L

Due Date: _____

Assigned To: _____

Resources Needed: _____

_____

_____

_____

Notes: _____

_____

_____

_____

_____

_____

_____

PLANNING: PRODUCTS AND SERVICES

Consider Flat Fee Pricing

There are several kinds of flat fee pricing. The most common example you see is the subscription model for services. Everything from Amazon Prime to unlimited car washes is sold on a subscription basis these days. Consider what you can offer this way.

Another common example is project labor. If a project is expected to bring in a certain amount from labor, you should always offer the client a flat fee proposal. Just be aware that cost overruns are your problem, and you might lose money if you don't manage the project well. But you can also make extra money by managing the project well.

As always, bundles can be your best friend. If you combine products and services into a bundle, you can guarantee yourself a very good profit.

You'll need to revisit this from time to time.

Complete! _____

Priority: H   M   L

Due Date: _____

Assigned To: _____

Resources Needed: _____

_____

_____

Notes: _____

_____

_____

_____

_____

_____

_____

PLANNING: STRATEGY

What Do You Need to Learn to Start Selling Services?

Remember: You don't know what you don't know. In many aspects of your business, you need to figure out what you don't know. More specifically, what don't you know about the business you're about to get into?

If you haven't read up on the Dunning-Kruger Effect, I recommend that you do. It's an interesting phenomenon in which people feel the greatest confidence in their abilities when they are the least competent. It's a good thing to keep in mind: It will also keep your ego in check!

You wouldn't be starting a business if you didn't have faith in your abilities. You've probably spent a long time gaining the knowledge and skills you have. Taking on the burden of running a business will require you to continually sharpen those skills while learning a lot stuff as well.

Complete! _____

Priority: H   M   L

Due Date: _____

Assigned To: _____

Resources Needed: _____

_____

_____

_____

Notes: _____

_____

_____

_____

_____

_____

_____

PLANNING: FINANCES

What Happens to My 401(k) Or 403(b) When I Leave My Job?

You need to do some research here. Talk to your HR department. They should be able to educate you on your options. Obviously, I'm going to send you off to have another discussion with your favorite tax Adviser.

You may be able to leave your 401(k) or 403(b) where it is. You certainly have the right to roll it over tax free into an IRA. Once you move this money to an IRA, you can invest in almost anything inside your IRA.

Another option is to cash out some or all of your retirement plan. Be aware that, if you are not of retirement age, you will pay a tax penalty and pay income tax (at your current rate). As a result, that should probably be your last resort.

Complete! _____

Priority: H   M   L

Due Date: _____

Assigned To: _____

Resources Needed: _____

_____

_____

_____

Notes: _____

_____

_____

_____

_____

_____

_____

_____

Stage Two:
Launch

LAUNCH: FINANCES

Merchant Service to Take Credit/Debit Cards

Credit card processors are called "merchant service" providers. You need to find one. Luckily, there are many options.

Almost all merchant service providers will promise the lowest rate to take credit cards. Make a note to shop around after your first year is complete. Your bank will offer merchant services, but will probably not be the cheapest option.

"Easy" options that allow you to instantly take cards are often the most expensive. You are trading ease-of-use for money. In that sense, they could be a good place to start. But always ask about rates. There's so much money in the industry, almost everyone is paying more than they should!

Also note: Different cards will charge different rates. Think about mileage cards or hotel points cards. YOU are paying for those benefits with the higher rates you pay for those cards. There's nothing you can do about that, but you should be aware of it.

Note: See the "Planning" advice on buying bundled services. See also PCI Compliance.

Complete! _____

Priority: H   M   L

Due Date: _____

Assigned To: _____

Resources Needed: _____

_____

_____

Notes: _____

_____

_____

_____

_____

_____

_____

LAUNCH: FINANCES

PCI Compliance

You need to protect credit card information pursuant to PCI (Payment Card Industry) standards. There are many ways to take credit cards. The least automated options are the most insecure. For example, if clients email credit card forms to you – even if they are encrypted – you have that data on your computer systems.

The most automated options are hosted, and the credit cards are managed so that you never have access to your client's credit card information. Your card processor has to work hard to maintain PCI compliance, but you don't have to do much at all.

As a rule, you should try to use services that take care of this compliance automatically. Ask.

Complete! _____

Priority: H   M   L

Due Date: _____

Assigned To: _____

Resources Needed: _____

_____

_____

_____

Notes: _____

_____

_____

_____

_____

_____

_____

_____

LAUNCH: FINANCES

Bank Account for Business

You will need a business bank account. If you operate your business as a sole proprietorship under your personal social security number, then this account will be opened under your name, potentially with a DBA ("doing business as") your business name.

If you turn your business as some other entity (e.g., corporation or LLC), then you will use your federal EIN (Employer Identification Number) as your tax ID to open the bank account. With some banks, everyone who opens a business account is automatically offered a business credit card, payroll processing, and a line of credit.

The bank will not take these options away from you, so please do not commit yourself to these services right away. Only accept the offers you need.

Complete! _____

Priority: H   M   L

Due Date: _____

Assigned To: _____

Resources Needed: _____

_____

_____

_____

Notes: _____

_____

_____

_____

_____

_____

_____

LAUNCH: FINANCES

Bookkeeper / Bookkeeping Service

If you're good with math, and decent with finances, you can do about ninety percent of what needs to be done with the finances of your company. But there are some key things you need to leave in the hands of a professional bookkeeper.

Engage a bookkeeper early on so that your QuickBooks and chart of accounts are set up properly. Your bookkeeper will also be a good Adviser regarding business generally. After all, they've seen many more company financials than you ever will.

Beware that you do not turn over your finances to a bookkeeper and then fail to keep yourself informed. Make sure you understand everything that's being done inside your business – especially with finances. You can have someone else do the work, but delegate – do not abdicate.

Looking for a sample Chart of Accounts? See the downloads for this book at www.smallbizquickstart.com.

Complete! _____

Priority: H   M   L

Due Date: _____

Assigned To: _____

Resources Needed: _____

_____

_____

_____

Notes: _____

_____

_____

_____

_____

_____

_____

_____

LAUNCH: FINANCES

Initial Funding of Your Business

At some point you will have determined how much money you need to get started. It may be zero, or a small sum. But if you need serious startup money, determine the best way to get it.

This might be a business loan from your bank or a private equity company. It may also come from a business line of credit, probably through your bank.

Some people use their personal credit cards to fund their business startup. This is one of the most expensive ways to fund your business. Almost every other source of funding will have a much lower interest rate.

In some cases, you might also be eligible for government grants.

Actions: 1) Determine how much money you need. 2) Consider where you will get this start-up money.

Complete! _____

Priority: H   M   L

Due Date: _____

Assigned To: _____

Resources Needed: _____

_____

_____

_____

Notes: _____

_____

_____

_____

_____

_____

_____

LAUNCH: STRATEGY

Investors: How Many?

Will you be looking for investors? If so, you'll need to do quite a bit of work. You'll need a business plan with a budget. You'll need to know how much money you need. If you are looking for funding in stages, you'll need to be clear about what you need for each stage.

How many investors do you want? It might be a few large investors or many small investors. If you're willing to try crowd funding, you may end up with lots of very small investors.

Finally, what do your investors get? In the classical investor model, you will be selling stock in your company. That means your investors get to own a piece of your business. Obviously engage professional advisers for this. With crowdfunding, you can simply pre-sell goods and services and retain ownership of your own company.

Note: Please see my Kindle Book entitled *Business Plan in a Month* for only 99¢. Check it out. Just go to Amazon and search for Palachuk *Business Plan in a Month*.

Complete! _____

Priority: H   M   L

Due Date: _____

Assigned To: _____

Resources Needed: _____

_____

_____

_____

Notes: _____

_____

_____

_____

_____

_____

_____

LAUNCH: FINANCES

Business Licenses and Other Licenses

Most state governments have a web site to help you figure out all the licenses and permits you need to run your business from home or within a specific city or county.

You will probably need a business license. This may be at the city or county level.

Once you start with the business license, you are likely to find a good resource for all the other local licenses and permits required in your area.

Some kinds of work require specific licenses. If you go into peoples' homes, you may need additional licensing for that.

Action: Google "Start a business in [your city] [your county] [your state]."

Complete! _____

Priority: H   M   L

Due Date: _____

Assigned To: _____

Resources Needed: _____

_____

_____

_____

Notes: _____

_____

_____

_____

_____

_____

_____

LAUNCH: FINANCES

Take Payments Any Way You Can

Elsewhere we discuss credit cards and merchant services. Please don't argue that you can't afford 2% on credit cards. It's 100% better than collecting old debts!

Some clients will want to pay by ACH (Automated Clearing House). Others by SWIFT (Society for Worldwide Interbank Financial Telecommunication) transfer or other bank transfer. And, more and more, PayPal is being used by businesses.

Many businesses still pay by check, so you should expect that as well.

These services may cost a little or a lot, so you'll need to do your research. Also, some will have transaction fees. If you have a lot of transactions, you should avoid transaction fees.

But the bottom line is: Some people will only pay by their favorite method. You need to let them pay you by that method!

Complete! _____

Priority: H   M   L

Due Date: _____

Assigned To: _____

Resources Needed: _____

_____

_____

Notes: _____

_____

_____

_____

_____

_____

_____

LAUNCH: FINANCES / STRATEGY / TAXES, ETC

Get a Good Tax Adviser

You will spend a lot of time in your company dealing with taxes. You will certainly have federal taxes. You may have state taxes. And there are probably small license fees at the local level.

In addition to all that, there may be payroll taxes, corporate taxes, sales tax, and more.

A tax Adviser is normally whoever does your taxes. That might be your accountant, an enrolled agent, or your bookkeeper. When it comes to tax advice, you need to find someone who is very good, and someone you can trust.

This may become one of the most important relationships you build in your business.

Complete! _____

Priority: H   M   L

Due Date: _____

Assigned To: _____

Resources Needed: _____

_____

_____

_____

Notes: _____

_____

_____

_____

_____

_____

_____

LAUNCH: STRATEGY

Articles of Incorporation, Bylaws, Amendments, Stock, etc.

When it's time to launch your corporation (should you choose to take that route), you will need to draft articles of incorporation and bylaws. You'll need to keep track of all corporation-related activity. If you have one or more partners or co-owners, then you will also need to track stock shares.

A great source for all this paperwork and advice on managing it is Nolo Press. They have books for forming your corporation. They have similar materials for non-profit corporations, and for inventions, trademarks, patents, etc.

I recommend you create a physical binder to store all this information. You won't need it often after your Launch, but you will need it occasionally.

See https://www.nolo.com/.

Complete! _____

Priority: H   M   L

Due Date: _____

Assigned To: _____

Resources Needed: _____

_____

_____

_____

Notes: _____

_____

_____

_____

_____

_____

LAUNCH: STRATEGY

DBA

DBA stands for "Doing Business As." No matter how you are organized (e.g., sole proprietor, corporation), you can use a DBA. For example, I started as a sole proprietor (Karl W. Palachuk) DBA KPEnterprises, and moved to a corporation, KPEnterprises Business Consulting, Inc. Today my corporation is Great Little Book Publishing Co., Inc., but I have a DBA for Small Biz Thoughts and another for Relax Focus Succeed™.

Depending on where your business is located, you may get your DBA from a county or a city office, or someplace else. Wherever you get your business license, someone will know where you go next to get your DBA. It may be the same office, or it may not.

In most locales, you will need to do some research to make sure no one else is using the company name you intend to use. And you will probably need to publish your DBA in a newspaper to inform the world that you are operating under this name.

Complete! _____

Priority: H   M   L

Due Date: _____

Assigned To: _____

Resources Needed: _____

_____

_____

_____

Notes: _____

_____

_____

_____

_____

_____

_____

LAUNCH: STRATEGY

Forming Your Company

For the life of your business, you will need to fill out forms that ask the "form" of your company.

The most common options are: Sole proprietorship, Partnership, Limited liability company (LLC), Corporation, and Cooperative (co-op). For corporations, you may choose between C-corp, S-corp, Non-Profit, or other specific types.

There are advantages and disadvantages to each of these. Everyone you meet will tell you tales about company forms that they've seen work and fail over the years.

When it's time to launch your business, you need to execute one of these. You can always revisit your decision, but you have to do something the first year.

Complete! _____

Priority: H   M   L

Due Date: _____

Assigned To: _____

Resources Needed: _____

_____

_____

_____

Notes: _____

_____

_____

_____

_____

_____

_____

_____

LAUNCH: INSURANCE

Insurance: Liability / General Business

The most basic insurance you need is simply "general" business insurance. This covers your liability in case something goes wrong and someone sues your company. There are many varieties of liability insurance. Ask your insurance agent or broker about what you need.

For example, you may need product liability in case something you produce might harm your customers. If you have employees, they might accidently hurt someone. When you think about liability, try to remember all the weird stories you've heard that ended with the phrase, "You can't make this stuff up."

Note: You may be able to combine many kinds of liability insurance into one policy. Find an insurance broker who can help you buy what you need. Note: You will revisit this discussion in a year.

Complete! _____

Priority: H   M   L

Due Date: _____

Assigned To: _____

Resources Needed: _____

_____

_____

Notes: _____

_____

_____

_____

_____

_____

_____

LAUNCH: INSURANCE

Insurance: Business Interruption

Most small businesses never think about business interruption insurance. When you start out, you aren't making any money. But soon your business will be making good money. What happens if you are shut down due to a hazmat spill or data corruption?

If you cannot operate your business, this insurance kicks it. Because such incidents are extremely rare, the insurance is generally not very expensive.

It may be built into your general business insurance. Ask.

Complete! _____

Priority: H   M   L

Due Date: _____

Assigned To: _____

Resources Needed: _____

_____

_____

_____

Notes: _____

_____

_____

_____

_____

_____

_____

LAUNCH: INSURANCE

Insurance: Commercial Property

You may not need property insurance at first. There are two reasons for this. First, you will probably have only a small amount of property inside your business. Second, this property might be covered by some other insurance, such as your homeowner's policy or your auto policy.

If you are in manufacturing or need to have a lot of specialized equipment, then you will need property insurance as soon as you acquire the equipment.

Again: Contact your insurance agent and share what you're doing now and where you're going.

Complete! _____

Priority: H   M   L

Due Date: _____

Assigned To: _____

Resources Needed: _____

_____

_____

_____

Notes: _____

_____

_____

_____

_____

_____

_____

LAUNCH: INSURANCE

Insurance: Errors and Omissions

Errors and Omissions – E&O – is a specific kind of liability insurance. It covers mistakes you might make as a professional. If you drop something on a client's foot, that would be covered under standard liability insurance. If you make a mistake in programming or analysis, your error might cost your client a lot of money. That would be covered by E&O insurance.

Ask your insurance agent whether E&O is already included in your general liability policy. It is also useful to talk about the kind of work you will be doing so you can buy the right amount of coverage.

Complete! _____

Priority: H   M   L

Due Date: _____

Assigned To: _____

Resources Needed: _____

_____

_____

_____

Notes: _____

_____

_____

_____

_____

_____

_____

Key Man (Officer & Director)

If your business is just you, and it will die when you do, then you don't need key man insurance. Similarly, if your company is large and every element of your position is well documented, then you may not need insurance because the company will continue fine if you were to disappear.

But if you have a larger organization that still relies on one (or a few) people to provide creativity and talent that cannot be easily replaced, then the company may be in serious trouble if something happens to the leadership.

As with all insurance, you need to decide whether you have enough at risk to make the insurance worthwhile.

Complete! _____

Priority: H   M   L

Due Date: _____

Assigned To: _____

Resources Needed: _____

_____

_____

_____

Notes: _____

_____

_____

_____

_____

_____

_____

LAUNCH: INSURANCE

Long Term Care or Disability

If you have long-term or disability insurance, make arrangements to continue this insurance as you leave employment and move into self-employment. You'll always be able to acquire long term insurance, but the price will be better before you are self-employed.

If you do not have long-term or disability insurance, sign up for it before you leave your job.

And, if you've already left or been laid off, please just bite the bullet and pay what you need to. You have no idea what the future holds. A long term illness or disability can bankrupt you, no matter how much money you have.

. . . And plan to revisit this topic in a year to compare pricing.

Complete! _____

Priority: H   M   L

Due Date: _____

Assigned To: _____

Resources Needed: _____

_____

_____

_____

Notes: _____

_____

_____

_____

_____

_____

_____

_____

LAUNCH: INSURANCE

Insurance: Personal Health + Dental

Personal health care and dental insurance are addressed in the Planning tasks. Now it's time to execute the decisions you made.

If you have insurance you wish to continue, then arrange for Cobra coverage. If you do not have insurance through your old job, you probably have insurance that will simply continue. Make sure you know for sure.

Document this decision: What is your personal health insurance? What is your dental insurance?

Complete! _____

Priority: H   M   L

Due Date: _____

Assigned To: _____

Resources Needed: _____

_____

_____

_____

Notes: _____

_____

_____

_____

_____

_____

_____

LAUNCH: INSURANCE

Insurance: Personal - Life

Strictly speaking, your personal life insurance is outside the business side of this discussion. But if you have a reason to insure your life, you should. If you have no spouse or dependent minor children, then you probably have no reason to maintain insurance that replaces your income.

If you do have a reason to insure your life, consider how your new business (and projected income) affect the size of your insurance policy.

As always, sit down with your insurance agent and make sure you're buying the right thing. And plan to revisit this discussion in a year.

Complete! _____

Priority: H M L

Due Date: _____

Assigned To: _____

Resources Needed: _____

_____

_____

_____

Notes: _____

_____

_____

_____

_____

_____

_____

LAUNCH: INSURANCE

Insurance: Umbrella Policy

As long as you're talking to your insurance agent, ask about an umbrella policy. If you are a sole proprietor or the owner (possibly with your spouse) of a closely held corporation, you may be able to combine the liability insurance for your cars, business, and even rental properties into one big umbrella policy.

Once you are committed to buying several kinds of liability insurance, a one (or two) million dollar liability umbrella policy will seem very affordable. And you may sleep better at night.

Complete! _____

Priority: H   M   L

Due Date: _____

Assigned To: _____

Resources Needed: _____

_____

_____

_____

Notes: _____

_____

_____

_____

_____

_____

_____

LAUNCH: INSURANCE

Insurance: Workers Comp

If you have employees, you will need to buy Workers Compensation insurance. This is basically insurance for on-the-job injuries suffered by your employees. The cost is determined by the category your workers are classified under. As you can imagine, people working on roofs with power tools are far more expensive to insure than people hunched over computer screens all day.

Lesson: Make sure your employee classifications are correct and cannot be challenged by the insurer when there's a claim. The right classifications can save you a great deal of money.

And here's some good news: As an owner (a principle) in the business with your own separate health insurance, you can exclude yourself from WC insurance. This will save you some money. If you do not fill out the paperwork properly, you will not be excluded. So just read carefully.

Complete! _____

Priority: H   M   L

Due Date: _____

Assigned To: _____

Resources Needed: _____

_____

_____

Notes: _____

_____

_____

_____

_____

_____

_____

LAUNCH: MARKETING

Get Business Cards.
Skip Stationery and Envelopes For Now

Business cards are probably the cheapest, best investment you can make in marketing. Don't be cheap in their creation or distribution. Print up nice cards and give them to everyone you can.

Pet peeve: Do not print your cards sideways or in odd shapes. There are two types of people who will take your card: Those who will throw it away and those who will actually use it. Those who use it will want it to be readable, scannable, and fit into a nice system with all the other business cards they collect. This rant is much longer on my blog. You can enjoy it here: https://blog.smallbizthoughts.com/search?q=business+cards

At least at the beginning, there is no need to print stationery or envelopes. When the time comes that you really need nice, expensive stationery, go get it printed. But don't do it just because people used to always do that before you were born.

Complete! _____

Priority: H   M   L

Due Date: _____

Assigned To: _____

Resources Needed: _____

_____

_____

_____

Notes: _____

_____

_____

_____

_____

_____

_____

LAUNCH: MARKETING

Consider a Launch Party

In the 21st century, you may have a "virtual" business with clients all over the country or the world. But it's still worth considering a launch party.

Gather all your friends together. Pick a theme and make a party out of it. Send out a press release. Give a quick speech that friends can stream on social media.

Celebrate your new adventure – and let your friends share in your celebration. Use it for public relations, but mostly enjoy the launching of the next stage in your (work) life!

Complete! _____

Priority: H   M   L

Due Date: _____

Assigned To: _____

Resources Needed: _____

_____

_____

_____

Notes: _____

_____

_____

_____

_____

_____

_____

LAUNCH: FINANCES / TAXES, ETC

Federal EIN (Tax ID)

You need an EIN – Employer Identification Number – even if you will never have employees. It is simply the number Uncle Sam uses to tax your business. And you want to be taxed appropriately, don't you?

Browse to www.irs.gov and search for form SS-4. You can submit the form online and you will probably get a response within eight business hours.

You should get an EIN as soon as you can. First, get a business license, then form your business (S-corp, etc.), THEN get your EIN. After that you can get a DBA if you need one, and open a bank account. Notice the building blocks here. All of this can be done in a day or two.

Complete! _____

Priority: H   M   L

Due Date: _____

Assigned To: _____

Resources Needed: _____

_____

_____

_____

Notes: _____

_____

_____

_____

_____

_____

_____

LAUNCH: FINANCES / TAXES, ETC

Sales and Use Tax / Reseller Certification

Different states use different names for a seller's permit. Basically, if you operate in a state that requires you to collect sales tax and submit it to the state, you need a seller's permit or reseller certification. This allows you to buy from suppliers without paying the sales tax.

Sales tax is collected only once, from the end user customer. So you, the "middle man" are not required to also pay sales tax.

Generally, there are three things you can do with merchandise you buy tax free. 1) You can mark it up and sell it for more money. You collect sales tax on the final price. 2) You can combine it with other things to create a taxable product. Again, you collect tax on the retail price. 3) You can use the merchandise inside your company, in which case you must declare this and pay a use tax equivalent to the sales tax.

Complete! _____

Priority: H   M   L

Due Date: _____

Assigned To: _____

Resources Needed: _____

_____

_____

_____

Notes: _____

_____

_____

_____

_____

_____

_____

LAUNCH: TECHNOLOGY

Data Storage, Sharing

The data within your company will become extremely valuable. If you lose this data and cannot recover it, the loss could be catastrophic. Most businesses that lose all of their data never recover and are forced to shut down.

Set up your data storage and sharing for your company. You might choose Dropbox, Microsoft Azure, Google Docs, JungleDisk, or a thousand other options. But you should find one primary place where you will store all company data.

You need to create a standard operating procedure for letting employees (and, potentially, contractors) access this data. You need to keep it safe when an employee leaves. However you do that, document it!

And you need to back up the data to another location in case something happens at the primary location. Do not assume your data is being backed up automatically. That almost never happens.

Ask a professional technology consultant to help you set this up the right way – and show you how to test your backups every month. Yes, that will cost money. But it will save you a lot in the long run!

Complete! _____

Priority: H   M   L

Due Date: _____

Assigned To: _____

Resources Needed: _____

_____

_____

_____

Notes: _____

_____

_____

_____

_____

_____

_____

_____

LAUNCH: TECHNOLOGY

Register Your Domain Name

You need an email address that represents you. You also need a web site. Do not use a generic email (such as Gmail) for your business. One key component of your email and your web site is your domain name.

There's no shortage of advice online about picking a domain name, so I'll just say one thing: The simpler and more obvious, the better.

Get your domain name as soon as you can. You'll need that email address for a lot of the forms you'll need to fill out.

Complete! _____

Priority: H   M   L

Due Date: _____

Assigned To: _____

Resources Needed: _____

_____

_____

_____

Notes: _____

_____

_____

_____

_____

_____

_____

LAUNCH: TECHNOLOGY

Get QuickBooks and Other Tools

Which tools do you need to run your business? At a minimum, you need a finance tool to send invoices, record payments, and generally "keep" your books. The most popular is QuickBooks. I know very few people who love QuickBooks. But it integrates with almost everything, and they have no real competition.

You may also need a CRM (customer relationship management) tool, a sales tracking tool, or a service delivery tool. In the IT business, we refer to these as "Line of Business" applications. There are applications for running a dental office, a construction company, a computer store, and pretty much any other business you can imagine.

Some of these tools are expensive, so people put off buying them. At some point, good tools will save you so much money that you will be sorry you waited so long. So don't wait so long. Plan to get good tools as soon as you can.

Complete! _____

Priority: H   M   L

Due Date: _____

Assigned To: _____

Resources Needed: _____

_____

_____

_____

Notes: _____

_____

_____

_____

_____

_____

_____

_____

LAUNCH: FINANCES / TAXES, ETC

How Will You Pay Yourself – Payroll Or Distributions?

If you are a sole proprietor, you will almost certainly pay yourself by simply taking distributions from the company. This can be as simple as transferring money from your business account to your personal account. But please do not use your business as an ATM, moving money around whenever you feel like it. That can raise a lot of red flags, not least of which with taxing agencies.

If you have an S-Corp (or LLC, or some other entity that files taxes as a corporation), you can pay yourself through payroll very easily. This allows you to easily make some estimated tax payments – at least for the payroll portion of your business. But you should also plan on having profit in your business, and that will flow to your personal taxes.

In other words, with a corporation or similar entity, there will still be "owner distributions" from the company to your personal account. Please track this stuff very carefully. At tax time, your tax pro will need to know how much you've paid in estimated tax payments, and what your company profit is.

Consult your tax pro and set up whatever systems they recommend – by the end of the first month of operating your business!

Complete! _____

Priority: H   M   L

Due Date: _____

Assigned To: _____

Resources Needed: _____

_____

_____

_____

Notes: _____

_____

_____

_____

_____

_____

_____

Stage Three: Year One

YEAR ONE: STRATEGY

Join These Communities

One of the "truths" you hear over and over about self-employment is that it can be lonely. And while that's true, loneliness won't kill your business. But isolation could! No matter how much you dislike a job, you have co-workers and people to talk to you. There are communities. And when you leave employment, you will also leave these communities.

It's up to you to find, join, or create communities that can constantly invigorate your business. Some communities might be local such as Meetup.com groups or a "mastermind" group of local business owners. Also join online groups. Some of these will be hosted on sites such as LinkedIn or Facebook. Others will be industry-specific. Plan to attend conferences within your industry.

When you consider all of these groups together, you will find your community of friends and mentors. Inside your community, you will be able to stay up to date with the challenges and opportunities within your industry. And, most importantly, it's a place where you can exchange ideas with other professionals and learn about new ways they are operating their businesses.

Complete! _____

Priority: H   M   L

Due Date: _____

Assigned To: _____

Resources Needed: _____

_____

_____

_____

Notes: _____

_____

_____

_____

_____

_____

_____

YEAR ONE: STRATEGY

Trade Associations, Magazines, And Podcasts

You are probably aware of the major professional associations in your industry. You should be a member or associate of some or all of these. If an association is free, or not very expensive, you should just join. If a membership is significantly expensive, you should pay attention and take part in whatever components you can afford.

Today, it is common for these associations to have free, cheap, and full-price options. Join all the newsletters. You may not have time to read through them all, but you need to spend some time "keeping up" with your industry. Be sure to filter these newsletters into a common folder. Whenever you get overwhelmed with the amount of information there, just delete them all and don't worry about it – there will be more newsletters tomorrow.

Similar to associations, you should find and subscribe to industry magazines, blogs, and podcasts. Most of these will be free. But some of the paid options may make sense as well. Again, you need to spend time immersing yourself in the industry you've chosen.

Complete! _____

Priority: H   M   L

Due Date: _____

Assigned To: _____

Resources Needed: _____

_____

_____

_____

Notes: _____

_____

_____

_____

_____

_____

_____

YEAR ONE: STRATEGY

Privacy - Contact Info, Financial Info

You've seen the news: "Personal Data" stolen from . . . [insert a large company or government office here]. How does that happen?

Well, there are billions of evil data-seeking digital robots scouring the Internet for data. Really: This is not an exaggeration. And while they're not "looking" for you, they weren't looking for Target or Facebook either. These robots simply attack every port on every single machine they can find on the Internet. And they steal anything that looks like a name, social security number, address, phone number, or mother's maiden name.

No matter what industry you're in, you will need to manage client-related information. There are many laws (and more on the way) to regulate how you handle client information. This includes financial information, as you would expect, but many other kinds of information as well.

Make every attempt to collect and store as little data as possible. At some point you have to have client names and data on your system. Do everything you can to secure it, and be prepared to let people know if it's stolen. Get an IT professional to help you do this right!

The best way to address this is to not have this information on your computers if you can avoid it. That means keeping it on a service for your invoicing or point of sale. They will have to secure their services, but they have a much larger budget and a much better chance than you of securing it.

Complete! _____

Priority: H   M   L

Due Date: _____

Assigned To: _____

Resources Needed: _____

_____

Notes: _____

_____

_____

_____

_____

Org Chart - Today And Future

Your organizational chart will change over time no matter what you do – including staying a sole proprietor who never hires employees. Start by drawing boxes to represent the roles you play (or the "hats" you wear): Sales, administration, service delivery, customer relations, etc.

Yes, your name is in every box. That's okay. Figure out all the roles you play. Over time, you'll figure out how much time you spend in each. Over time, you will also add more roles to your org chart. Maybe you'll even share a box with a contractor or employee some time.

Re-visit your org chart at least once a year. At some point it will grow to include other people. They might be services, such as bookkeeping or marketing. Or they might be employees. Eventually, the boxes will have roles assigned to names other than your own.

Complete! _____

Priority: H   M   L

Due Date: _____

Assigned To: _____

Resources Needed: _____

_____

_____

_____

Notes: _____

_____

_____

_____

_____

_____

_____

_____

YEAR ONE: EMPLOYEES

Job Descriptions – Current and Future Employees

When it's time to hire your first employee, it's also time to start defining specific job roles. Over time, to be truly successful, you need to define job descriptions separate from the people who currently occupy a specific role.

Remember: If your business is successful, people will leave. That's okay. In fact, it's good. Life goes on. People get married, fall in love, move away, or just decide that they want to take another job. That means you need to define each job so you can figure out who to hire when someone leaves.

Do not design your business around specific people who just happen to be working for you today.

Eventually, you'll be able to write a job description for each role in your company. From there, you'll write a job advertisement and the evaluation sheet for interviewing candidates. That, in turn, will give you the criteria for quarterly goals and quarterly evaluations.

Don't worry about this. Just do it and let it evolve over time. Eventually, you'll have a consistent process that flows from job description to employee evaluation.

Complete! _____

Priority: H   M   L

Due Date: _____

Assigned To: _____

Resources Needed: _____

_____

_____

_____

Notes: _____

_____

_____

_____

_____

_____

_____

YEAR ONE: EMPLOYEES

Training Manual

It's always good to document your processes. As you begin to engage others to help you in your business, you need to document every job and every process, no matter how small. I recommend you start with a common folder and create individual task documents.

You should also create a "Who-What" document that defines who (which job description) does each task (what) in your company. So, for example, if you wonder who should be processing daily updates to a program, you can quickly find out which role is responsible for that.

Eventually, you'll be able to gather together all the tasks assigned to a specific role. That becomes one section in your training manual. Or, alternatively, it becomes the training manual for the next person you hire into to that job.

Remember: The last item on every checklist is "Update the checklist."

Complete! _____

Priority: H   M   L

Due Date: _____

Assigned To: _____

Resources Needed: _____

_____

_____

_____

Notes: _____

_____

_____

_____

_____

_____

_____

_____

YEAR ONE: FINANCES

EBITDA - Learn It and Set Targets

EBITDA – Earnings before interest, taxes, dividends, and amortization – is a universal standard for the profitability of your company. Make sure you ask your tax Adviser to explain it to you, and keep going until you actually understand it.

Traditional wisdom is that your EBITDA should be at least 10-12%. That means that your actual profit is 10-12% of your revenue. So, if your revenue is $500,000 and your profit is 10%, your profit will equal $50,000.

You might be saying, "WHAT? How can I live on $50,000?" Well, you can't. EBITDA needs to be the profit *after* you pay yourself. In other words, it's the real, actual profit after you take home a reasonable salary. The reason for this is simple. As a somewhat universal measure of profit, EBITDA is a critical element in measuring the potential value of your company if you were to sell it. If that happens, someone else will take your job, and your salary, and the company needs to be just as profitable.

EBITDA is a number that will change over time. With luck, it will grow much larger than 12%.

Complete! _____

Priority: H   M   L

Due Date: _____

Assigned To: _____

Resources Needed: _____

_____

_____

_____

Notes: _____

_____

_____

_____

_____

_____

_____

_____

Year One: Finances

Next Level Monthly Financials

Once you start operating your business, you need to keep QuickBooks (or whatever you use) up to date – to the day and the hour if possible. As time goes on, you'll be able to run reports to determine what actually happened in each month of the year. The easiest report of this is your P&L – profit and loss report.

I highly recommend that you create an Excel spreadsheet that simply recreates this P&L and that you fill in all the rows each month with real numbers. For columns, enter the months themselves (Jan, Feb, Mar, etc.). At the top of each column write either Actual or Projected. When the numbers before real, label them as Actual. All months after that are projected.

Taken as a whole, this spreadsheet represents your projected income and expenses for the year. And, of course, your profit. While I discourage you from constantly making changes to your projections, you should update your projections about two or three times during the year. Make them as real as possible, so you can plan based on the best information you have.

Complete! _____

Priority: H   M   L

Due Date: _____

Assigned To: _____

Resources Needed: _____

_____

_____

_____

Notes: _____

_____

_____

_____

_____

_____

_____

YEAR ONE: FINANCES

Understand and Make Quarterly Tax Payments

The IRS requires that you make tax payments in a "timely" manner. If you are a sole proprietor or do not pay yourself a salary (via W2), that means you need to magically know what your profit will be at the end of the year, and pay 25% of your taxes every quarter until you reach the end of the year.

Given that that's impossible, here's what you actually do:

Browse to IRS.gov and search for form 1040-ES. That form includes a worksheet to estimate your income and your taxes. It also lists the specific filing dates to file your payments (April 15, June 15, September 15, and January 15 of the next year).

Note that you may also pay yourself via W2 as an employer. This is a good way to make sure most of your taxes are taken care of. But you will need to track taxes paid via payroll and make a best-guess estimate of what you need to pay via quarterly estimates. Don't freak out. Communicate frequently with your tax adviser and keep tweaking the process. In the end, the amount you pay will be the same.

Complete! _____

Priority: H   M   L

Due Date: _____

Assigned To: _____

Resources Needed: _____

_____

_____

_____

Notes: _____

_____

_____

_____

_____

_____

_____

YEAR ONE: FINANCES

Establish Good Collection Processes and Policies

Eventually, you will have rational terms of service and collections processes. That means: 1) You will get paid in advance as often as possible; 2) You will charge late fees and interest for late payments; and 3) You will cut off services to clients who do not pay.

Too many people start their businesses by giving terms that no one asked for, and forgiving clients who don't pay you. The longer you are in business, the more likely it is that you will be tired of this abuse and simply stop putting up with it.

Here's a better idea: Start out doing it the right way. Have reasonable terms and enforce them from the start. This is the way business is done. Learn how to do it in Year One, not year ten or twenty.

Complete! _____

Priority: H   M   L

Due Date: _____

Assigned To: _____

Resources Needed: _____

_____

_____

_____

Notes: _____

_____

_____

_____

_____

_____

_____

_____

YEAR ONE: FINANCES

File Sales Tax Returns

Earlier, we warned you that you'll need to files sales tax returns. This becomes real when you open your doors and start selling things. Depending on your state, and your sales volume, you may need to file sales tax returns monthly or quarterly.

However you do it, you need to figure out how to track everything that's subject to sales tax. If you're lucky and have the right advice, you may figure out how to track this inside a tool such as QuickBooks. Until you figure that out, you need to find another way to track taxable sales.

Almost all state sales tax web sites do a good job of helping you to get this right. So create the accounts you need and make sure you make your payments in a timely manner.

Complete! _____

Priority: H   M   L

Due Date: _____

Assigned To: _____

Resources Needed: _____

_____

_____

Notes: _____

_____

_____

_____

_____

_____

_____

YEAR ONE: EMPLOYEES

NDA For Employees, Staff, And Clients

Google "Non-Disclosure Agreement" and you'll find lots of examples of language for your NDAs. As you add these to contracts and employee agreements, ask a lawyer to go over them and verify that they are enforceable in your state. Even if they're perfect, your lawyer is required to make at least a small change in order to justify their fee. (That's a smart-ass comment, but it's still true.)

Assuming you have developed processes and procedures about how you run your company, you will need to protect your intellectual property by having your employees and contractors sign NDAs. You also need to protect your clients' IP (intellectual property). I recommend you have employees sign an NDA on the day your hire them, and to renew it each January. Keep these in a folder.

Your client contracts should include a two-way NDA, protecting both your intellectual property and that of your clients. As a sales point, be sure to tell your clients that every one of your employees signs an NDA that covers their IP as well.

Complete! _____

Priority: H   M   L

Due Date: _____

Assigned To: _____

Resources Needed: _____

_____

_____

_____

Notes: _____

_____

_____

_____

_____

_____

_____

YEAR ONE: MARKETING

A Regular Newsletter Is Your Best Friend

The absolute greatest marketing asset you will develop in your business is your newsletter mailing list. Love this list, grow this list, and respect this list. Do not abuse it by over-using it. But do send a good newsletter that brings value and gets people to think.

Your newsletter list should include all of your clients (and as many of their employees as you can) as well as your prospects, and anyone else who wants to receive your newsletter. Tie all "freebie" give-aways and web site forms to your newsletter list. Grow your list at every opportunity.

The newsletter should be at least monthly, if not weekly. The newsletter should represent YOU and your approach to everything. Make it interesting, useful, and motivational. Put true value into every newsletter and people will open it every time it lands in their mailbox.

Complete! _____

Priority: H   M   L

Due Date: _____

Assigned To: _____

Resources Needed: _____

_____

_____

_____

Notes: _____

_____

_____

_____

_____

_____

_____

_____

YEAR ONE: MARKETING

It's All About You. Be Your Brand.

One of the perennial topics you'll see in business is the discussion of your USP – Unique Selling Proposition. In other words, what makes your company different? What's the value you bring to clients? This is used as the basis for a discussion of why clients should do business with you.

Let me make your life easy: Your USP is YOU! Embrace this concept and you will save hundreds of hours and thousands of dollars over the years. Are you conservative or liberal? Quiet or outspoken? Spiritual? Professional? Whatever you are, be that and find clients who want to do business with you.

Too many businesses waste too much time trying to execute someone else's formula for success. A much better strategy is to figure out how to add your personal stamp to everything you do. What's your way of creating videos, delivering a presentation, or delivering a service of any kind?

You will read and hear an amazing amount of advice about how to run your business. In the end, you will be most successful doing things your way. After all, when you copy someone else, the best you can ever be is number two.

Complete! _____

Priority: H   M   L

Due Date: _____

Assigned To: _____

Resources Needed: _____

_____

_____

_____

Notes: _____

_____

_____

_____

_____

_____

_____

_____

YEAR ONE: MARKETING

Mailing Lists, Marketing, And More

There are hundreds (maybe thousands) of ways to market your company and your services. Your mailing list is the most important because you can have a never-ending conversation with your clients and prospects. But you will need to determine other ways to connect with prospects as well.

You cannot do it all. You can't even come close. Your first year should be dedicated to trying things to see if they work for you. Keep the ones that work and discard those that don't. You'll find that some marketing methods are not very fun, but they work for your business. Like it or not, you need to do more of those. At the same time, there might be things you like to do that simply don't bring in clients. You need to drop those.

This cycle (Try new things; keep what works; drop what doesn't) will be repeated endlessly for as long as you are in business. Don't begrudge it or neglect it. Embrace your marketing as a daily exercise habit that will keep your business healthy.

Complete! _____

Priority: H   M   L

Due Date: _____

Assigned To: _____

Resources Needed: _____

_____

_____

_____

Notes: _____

_____

_____

_____

_____

_____

_____

_____

YEAR ONE: MARKETING

Stationary, Envelopes, Etc.

In the "Launch" section I advised that you avoid creating stationary and customized envelopes until later. Here I would simply remind you to avoid this expense until it's absolutely necessary.

If you are doing a large mailing, that's a great time to order custom envelopes, and perhaps stationary. Order a few extras for a tiny amount of money. These days, 250 extra envelopes might last you for the next ten years – or until you create another large mailing.

Remember, you can create beautiful and colorful letterhead on your computer and send letters to clients in PDF format. So you may never actually need to create pre-printed stationary in the real world. The bottom line is: Don't spend money on this stuff because your grandfather did. If you don't need to spend the money, don't.

Complete! _____

Priority: H   M   L

Due Date: _____

Assigned To: _____

Resources Needed: _____

_____

_____

_____

Notes: _____

_____

_____

_____

_____

_____

_____

YEAR ONE: EMPLOYEES

Making Money with Outsource Labor

There's never been a better time to start a business. In addition to hiring people to work for you, you have the opportunity to engage millions of people working in the "gig" economy to provide products and services for your company. There are two ways to make money by outsourcing jobs.

First, you can engage people to do lots and lots of work for you. Google "virtual assistant" for a tip-of-the-iceberg view of what's possible. Then spend an afternoon browsing around Fiverr.com. And when you need larger engagements, check out Upwork.com.

A tiny list of things you can outsource includes administrative work, transcribing videos, social media management, marketing services, graphics, video production, newsletters, blogging, layout of printed materials, editing, proofreading, and web site design.

Second, you can outsource the actual work you sell. For many service industries, this is simply a matter of engaging a company that can provide work remotely and marking up their services. As for products, that's even easier. There is almost no limit to the products that you can resell under your name and have drop-shipped around the world. This bit of commerce is over 150 years old, but the Internet makes it easier than ever.

You might be able to expand your business significantly without having any actual employees in-house.

Complete! _____

Priority: H   M   L

Due Date: _____

Assigned To: _____

Resources Needed: _____

_____

Notes: _____

_____

_____

_____

_____

_____

YEAR ONE: EMPLOYEES

Part-time Employees

Too many people only think about "full time" or salaried employees when it's time to think about hiring someone. This is a very expensive route. I highly encourage you to start with a part-time worker who can commit ten or twenty hours per week. This makes it much easier to keep your cash flow under control. And, of course, you don't have to come up with the money for an annual salary plus taxes and related expenses.

Google "$200 Miracle" to find a much longer article I wrote about this. I've updated it a few times over the years, but the advice is all solid.

There are many, many people who want to work only 10-20 hours per week. These include students (both high school and college) as well as stay-at-home parents who want to take their kids to school in the morning, work during the day, and pick their kids up in the afternoon. These people are often very well educated, very talented, and often have great experience.

Never believe the argument that you are taking advantage of these people. You are helping them build their resume as well as their portfolio of achievements. Assume they will only stay a year or two and be grateful when someone stays five. In the meantime, help them build the credentials they need to get their next great job.

Complete! _____

Priority: H   M   L

Due Date: _____

Assigned To: _____

Resources Needed: _____

_____

Notes: _____

_____

_____

_____

_____

YEAR ONE: EMPLOYEES

Virtual Assistant (Or Non-Virtual)

Elsewhere we covered outsourcing and part-time employees. In most cases, I highly recommend that your first hire is an administrative assistant. This might be in-house (someone who shows up at your office) or an outsourced service.

Many business owners are tempted to hire someone to take care of the core functions of their business. In other words, they want to hire a "technician" who can do the work. That is often an expensive option, especially if the work you do is anything other than repetitive, unskilled labor.

An admin can take care of a huge number of tasks that take your time and provide very little direct benefit to your company. But the paperwork has to be done! And someone needs to check the mailbox, answer the phones, balance the checkbook, verify that orders are processed, send memos to clients, stuff envelopes, and a thousand little things.

And admin might take twenty hours to do the work you can do in ten. But that will still free you up to deliver ten more hours of the core labor that brings money to your company. This approach can allow you to expand your abilities significantly without hiring an expensive technician.

Complete! _____

Priority: H   M   L

Due Date: _____

Assigned To: _____

Resources Needed: _____

_____

_____

Notes: _____

_____

_____

_____

_____

_____

_____

YEAR ONE: STRATEGY

Create Cross-Checks for Everything

A really great habit to develop while you're doing everything you do in your business is to create cross-checks. It is most obvious that you need to do this with finances. No one other than the owner should be able to handle an entire chain of financial transactions without creating a way to track everything that is done. That's how you avoid embezzlement. It's also a good habit when it's just you, before you hire people to help you.

Here's an example: When we sell a product online, there's automatically a transaction in our online store. When we "process" this order, we enter the order information, including name, order number, and payment transaction ID into an Excel tracking sheet. Separately, there are entries into the merchant service account and QuickBooks. Again, these each provide transaction and invoice numbers, along with the customer name and possibly email. Finally, we track shipping information whether it's done automatically or we ship the order ourselves.

The goal is to have a way to quickly access any order, any QuickBooks entry, any customer, any tracking number, and so forth. This is far less complicated than it sounds. Just think about the few common entries that will quickly help you find the status of any order when a customer calls. Name, email, and order number are a great place to start.

Complete! _____

Priority: H M L

Due Date: _____

Assigned To: _____

Resources Needed: _____

_____

_____

Notes: _____

_____

_____

_____

_____

_____

YEAR ONE: STRATEGY

Coaches - Life, Business, Sales, etc.

There are coaches for almost everything you do in your business and they're available at almost any price point. I am a huge believer in coaching. I have paid for business coaches, sales coaches, life coaches, and even a speaking coach. Remember: Even the greatest athletes in the world have coaches. Even at the height of your career, there's always someone who can help you do better.

Beware of "coaching" programs that are really just sales pitches for a pre-recorded series of videos. Those might have value. In fact, they might be extremely valuable. But such programs are not coaching.

Coaching involves someone who can help you address the specific goals and challenges of your business. While more generic advice can be very valuable, coaching is intended to help you take your business (or personal life) to the next level.

My experience as both a coach and someone who hires coaches is that you will experience plateaus in coaching. Be aware that these will happen and don't give up just because you hit a plateau. Take a break, take a breath, and work with your coach to determine what your next level is.

Complete! _____

Priority: H   M   L

Due Date: _____

Assigned To: _____

Resources Needed: _____

_____

_____

_____

Notes: _____

_____

_____

_____

_____

_____

_____

YEAR ONE: PRODUCTS AND SERVICES

Standard Markup Pricing on Products

In almost any industry, there is a standard markup on products. This is simple to calculate. A three percent markup is determined by the wholesale price times 1.03. Ten percent markup is wholesale times 1.10. And so forth.

In general, it's great advice to completely ignore your competition, what they're doing, how they deliver services, and how they markup their merchandise. You cannot differentiate yourself by being exactly like your competition, only one percent cheaper.

I recommend that you set a healthy markup that guarantees you will be profitable. Early on in your business, that might mean that your retail price is higher than your competition – or even higher than what your customers can find online. Believe it or not, that's okay!

I always tell my clients that I will make sure that I sell them the right thing for their business. My prices are frequently a bit higher than retail – and much higher than what they can get on Amazon. Clients know they're paying a bit more, but they hold me 100% responsible if what I sell them isn't just right.

Complete! _____

Priority: H   M   L

Due Date: _____

Assigned To: _____

Resources Needed: _____

_____

_____

_____

Notes: _____

_____

_____

_____

_____

_____

_____

YEAR ONE: PRODUCTS AND SERVICES

Project Quoting, Planning, and Pricing

Managing projects profitably can be a serious challenge if you've never done it before. You may have delivered some or all of a project that was sold by someone in your company. Managing the whole thing from sales to delivery is a much bigger undertaking.

There are whole books written on project management. And maybe someday you'll have time to read one. But in the meantime, you need to create a simple tracking system to make sure that you quote projects profitably, manage them profitably, and use your tracking information to make sure you're even more accurate at quoting the next project.

I recommend a spreadsheet that allows you to create rows that flow from internal quote (not seen by client) to client quote, project tasks, and final targets. Make sure you track your time inside each task so that you know the true costs and profit for every piece of project. That will help you quote future projects.

If you need a starter spreadsheet for managing project flows, see the downloads for this workbook at SmallBizQuickstart.com.

Complete! _____

Priority:　H　　M　　L

Due Date: _____

Assigned To: _____

Resources Needed: _____

_____

_____

_____

Notes: _____

_____

_____

_____

_____

_____

_____

_____

YEAR ONE: PRODUCTS AND SERVICES

Quoting Projects

I highly recommend that you quote projects for a flat fee. The reasons are simple. First, clients hate to pay for the discovery and project planning stage. They'll say, "This project is so simple, we don't need a planning stage." I always use the analogy of building a house. They say they want a one-room cabin. When you deliver that, they ask where the bathroom is. And the bedroom. And the second story. The result is a project that is inefficient and looks glommed together.

Never let clients see the financial details or hours inside the project. For example, don't allocate X hours for setup and Y hours for creative work. If you do this, you run the risk that a client will say that you should rebate hours that were not used for a specific stage of the project.

If you figure out your internal cost, you can add ten percent for administrative overhead and give the client a flat-fee quote. That way, you get paid for the planning stage. And, even if you don't make money on one piece of the project, you might make extra money on another, and the whole project will be profitable.

If you need a starter spreadsheet for managing project flows, see the downloads for this workbook at SmallBizQuickstart.com.

Complete! _____

Priority: H   M   L

Due Date: _____

Assigned To: _____

Resources Needed: _____

_____

_____

Notes: _____

_____

_____

_____

_____

_____

_____

YEAR ONE: FINANCES

Office Space. Do You Need It? Store Front?

Before you run out and rent office space of any size, consider whether you really need it. If your business plan includes a storefront or a showroom, you obviously need to rent space. But if your work is done while you're alone and clients never visit your office, then it's highly unlikely that you need space outside your house.

Having said all that, you may have personal reasons to have an "outside" office. Perhaps you need business class Internet bandwidth, or you simply can't work at home without making four trips to the refrigerator every hour. Or perhaps the dog next door won't shut up and you make frequent phone calls.

Even a small room in a shared office space will cost $300 or $400 per month. Larger space can easily go to $1,000 or $1,500 for four bare walls. Those costs mount up very quickly once you start adding furniture, office supplies, and computer equipment.

The bottom line is: Try to work from home as long as you can. Once it's time to get an office, make sure you have a realistic budget.

Complete! _____

Priority: H   M   L

Due Date: _____

Assigned To: _____

Resources Needed: _____

_____

_____

_____

Notes: _____

_____

_____

_____

_____

_____

_____

YEAR ONE: STRATEGY

Manual of Processes and Procedures

Elsewhere we cover your training manual. That will be built from your SOPs (standard operating procedures). And your SOPs will be built from every single thing that needs to be done in your business. It is an absolute best practice to document everything you do.

Don't worry that this will take a great deal of time. When you create an invoice, for example, create a simple, one-page checklist on how you do that.

Some tasks are done every day and are easy to remember and execute consistently. Others are only done once a month or once a quarter. Those are harder to remember and creating a checklist is the only way to execute them the same way every time.

SOPs will make it much easier for you to hire employees and contractors, expand your business, provide consistently high levels of service, and someday open a branch office that operates as well as the original. Remember the simple reason Subway operates the largest food franchise in the world with a bunch of 18-year-olds: They have awesome SOPs!

Complete! _____

Priority: H   M   L

Due Date: _____

Assigned To: _____

Resources Needed: _____

_____

_____

_____

Notes: _____

_____

_____

_____

_____

_____

_____

YEAR ONE: STRATEGY

Tracking Time Inside Your Business

One of the key differentiators of people who excel at their chosen profession is their commitment to ongoing education. No profession, no matter how "un-technical" in nature, escapes evolution. Materials change all the time. Best practices are updated. As related industries change, changes in your industry are inevitable.

Of course you need to know what's going on in your industry. But you need to do more than that: you need to know what's coming next. And when things change, you need to embrace the new. Whether you consider yourself an "early adopter" or someone who waits until changes become mainstream, you need to accept the fact that your industry will continually change all the time, for as long as you're in business.

In addition to the core business you run, all the related businesses will also keep changing forever. Commit to continually updating your knowledge as the years roll on.

Complete! _____

Priority: H   M   L

Due Date: _____

Assigned To: _____

Resources Needed: _____

_____

_____

_____

Notes: _____

_____

_____

_____

_____

_____

_____

_____

YEAR ONE: STRATEGY / EMPLOYEES

Certifications. Yes or no?

Depending on your industry, there may be certifications available to you. These can range from technical certifications such as Microsoft or Cisco exams to vocational certifications for welding, photography, and thousands of other things.

You need to determine whether such certifications are good for your business, even if they are not required for government permits or compliance. You may be able to use these certs to differentiate yourself from less-motivated members of your profession. They may also be good for marketing purposes.

These certs are part of your professional growth strategy. If you do pursue them, be sure to add them to your resume and your LinkedIn profile. And remember: you can always start down the certification path. You don't have to do it right away. And you can always stop if it doesn't help your business.

Complete! _____

Priority: H   M   L

Due Date: _____

Assigned To: _____

Resources Needed: _____

_____

_____

_____

Notes: _____

_____

_____

_____

_____

_____

_____

YEAR ONE: STRATEGY

Become A Life-Long Learner – Especially in Your Profession

One of the key differentiators of people who excel at their chosen profession is their commitment to ongoing education. No profession, no matter how "un-technical" in nature, escapes evolution. Materials change all the time. Best practices are updated. As related industries change, changes in your industry are inevitable.

Of course you need to know what's going on in your industry. But you need to do more than that: you need to know what's coming next. And when things change, you need to embrace the new. Whether you consider yourself an "early adopter" or someone who waits until changes become mainstream, you need to accept the fact that your industry will continually change all the time, for as long as you're in business.

In addition to the core business you run, all the related businesses will also keep changing forever. Commit to continually updating your knowledge as the years roll on.

Complete! _____

Priority: H   M   L

Due Date: _____

Assigned To: _____

Resources Needed: _____

_____

_____

_____

Notes: _____

_____

_____

_____

_____

_____

_____

YEAR ONE: STRATEGY

Find Vendors Who Can Help You Make Money

"Vendor" is a fairly generic term that defines someone you buy stuff from. If you manufacture goods, vendors sell you the parts you need (or whole products you resell). Other people in your industry will use some or all of the same vendors.

If you use specialized software or special tools to run your company, the companies that create those things are also your vendors. Again, other people in your industry will use some or all of the same vendors.

Really good vendors will help you develop good relationships with them and with your clients. They will help you get certified in their products/services. They will help you market and advertise your company. They will do all kinds of things to help you to be successful. After all, the more successful you are, the more successful they are.

Find good vendors and be as loyal to them as they are to you.

Complete! _____

Priority: H   M   L

Due Date: _____

Assigned To: _____

Resources Needed: _____

_____

_____

_____

Notes: _____

_____

_____

_____

_____

_____

_____

YEAR ONE: STRATEGY

Find Good Distributors

One specialized type of vendor is a distributor. Distributors buy lots of different kinds of merchandise directly from manufacturers and sometimes from other specialty distributors. You need to be a reseller in order to buy from them. We call this buying wholesale.

Some manufacturers will only sell to you through a distributor, and some only if you are an "authorized" reseller (authorized through the manufacturer). There may be restrictions regarding training, territory, or importation limits. A good distributor will help you meet all these requirements so you can resell the specific products.

In many cases, you must commit to a specific sales volume as well. So, for example, if you can't sell $100,000 worth of the product in a year, then you will lose your right to resell it. Similarly, if you do reach certain thresholds, then you can move up to Silver, Gold, or Platinum partner status and receive additional discounts on the products you buy at wholesale.

As you can see, there can be a lot of profit added as you move from non-reseller, to reseller, to chosen reseller status for many manufacturers. But you rarely deal with them. Your relationship is probably with your distributor. So make sure you build that relationship.

Complete! _____

Priority: H   M   L

Due Date: _____

Assigned To: _____

Resources Needed: _____

_____

_____

Notes: _____

_____

_____

_____

_____

_____

_____

YEAR ONE: STRATEGY

Manufacturers, Suppliers

See also the discussion of distributors.

Some manufacturers or suppliers will sell to your directly. If you are creating a product, it is important to have good suppliers. What does "good" mean?

A good supplier will focus on quality. Quality parts make for quality products which, in turn, make for fewer problems and fewer returns. A good supplier will also be loyal to you over time when the market forces are difficult on small business and they're feeling pressure from newer, larger clients. Good suppliers will have good processes for ordering and shipping.

In every element of every business, there are low, medium, and high quality options. Whatever you decide to be, you need to find a supplier who is consistent with that. You can't build good products or good relationships with low quality manufacturers or suppliers.

If a specific resource is absolutely critical to your business, you should have two sources for it. That means you will not get the best prices from either because each will get about half your purchasing volume. But if something goes wrong with a source or a supplier, you will still have another option.

Complete! _____

Priority: H   M   L

Due Date: _____

Assigned To: _____

Resources Needed: _____

_____

_____

Notes: _____

_____

_____

_____

_____

_____

_____

YEAR ONE: FINANCES

Weekly Cash Flow Reports

In the Planning stage, we introduced you to cash flow. With luck, you created estimated cash flow projections for the first twelve months. Once your business is "real" it's time to create a weekly cash flow report to determine exactly how much money you have at your fingertips.

This is surprisingly easy. The formula is:

Money you have in your business bank account right now . . .

Plus money that you actually expect to come in within the next week . . .

Minus money that you will actually use to pay bills or payroll in the next week.

Notice that this is not all the money owed to you or all the money you owe to others. It's real world dollars that you really expect coming into and going out of your bank account. This is the pulse of money in your business. This weekly report should take about three minutes to put together.

Eventually you'll be able to do it off the top of your head by looking at your bank account. And, with luck, you'll get to the point where you run this report more than once a week. I do it almost every single day in my businesses.

For a sample weekly cash flow example, grab the downloads for this book at www.smallbizquickstart.com.

Complete! _____

Priority: H   M   L

Due Date: _____

Assigned To: _____

Resources Needed: _____

_____

Notes: _____

_____

_____

_____

_____

_____

YEAR ONE: INSURANCE

Annual Insurance Tune-Up

Other than the topic of "finance" generally, one of the most common topics has been insurance. There's insurance related to business, personal, clients, employees, medical, liability, and on and on. That's a lot of insurance. So, if you look at insurance as a whole, it makes great sense to look at it once a year and make sure you have the right policies at the right price.

You might divide this into several chores. Review workers comp in January, general business in February, group health in October, etc. And maybe some insurance is stable enough that you only want to review it once every three years. But, still write that into your calendar and make sure it gets done.

As California workers comp laws changed over the years, I have saved many thousands of dollars by reviewing our policies again and again. This is a great example of a chore that can be performed by your administrative assistant.

Insurance companies are a lot like the phone company or Internet service provider. They might offer a better, cheaper plan, but they will never tell you about it as long as you are on a worse, more expensive plan. Therefore, it's your job to go looking for the better plan.

Complete! _____

Priority: H   M   L

Due Date: _____

Assigned To: _____

Resources Needed: _____

_____

_____

Notes: _____

_____

_____

_____

_____

_____

_____

Good Luck!

Good Luck in Your New Business!

I will never forget the odd combination of fear and optimism when I quit my last "real" job and started my business. I went out in the world with a LOT less information than you have, if you've read through this workbook!

But like billions of people around the world and through the years, I figured it out. You can never be perfect or have perfect planning. But you can always go forth with a positive, can-do attitude.

I encourage you to practice some quiet time every day to think about your life and your business. Keep everything in perspective and keep moving forward. There will be challenges and victories. There will be hard times and good times.

But stick to it and you will understand and experience a level of self-reliance and fulfillment that can only come from running your own business. It's rarely easy. But the rewards to your mental health (and bank book) can be tremendous!

Good luck in your grand new adventure. And when you successfully Launch your business, send me an email to say, "I did it!"

Congratulations!

- karlp@smallbizthoughts.com

Resources

- American Arbitration Association at https://www.adr.org

- On Business Cards: https://blog.smallbizthoughts.com/search?q=business+cards

- Chandler, Stephanie, *The Business Startup Checklist and Planning Guide: Seize Your Entrepreneurial Dreams!*, Aventine Press, 2005.

- Dropbox storage. www.dropbox.com

- Fiverr.com

- Gerber, Michael E., *The E-Myth Revisited: Why Most Small Businesses Don't Work and What to Do About It*, Harper Business, 2004.

- Google Docs. https://docs.google.com

- JungleDisk storage. www.jungledisk.com

- Mandino, Og, *The Greatest Salesman in the World*, Bantam Doubleday Dell, 1972.

- Meetup.com

- Microsoft Azure. https://azure.microsoft.com

- NOLO Press. www.nolo.com

- Palachuk, Karl W., *The Absolutely Unbreakable Rules of Service Delivery*, Great Little Book Publishing Co., Inc., 2020.

- Palachuk, Karl W., *Business Plan in a Month*, Kindle Book, 2020.

- Palachuk, Karl W., *Relax Focus Succeed: Balance Your Personal and Professional Lives and Be More Successful in Both*, Revised Edition, 2013.

- Pressfield, Steven, *Turning Pro: Tap Your Inner Power and Create Your Life's Work*, Black Irish Entertainment LLC, 2012.

- Pressfield, Steven, *The War of Art: Break Through the Blocks and Win Your Inner Creative Battles*, Black Irish Entertainment LLC, 2012.

- Upwork.com

- U.S. Internal Revenue Service. www.IRS.gov

- U.S. Small Business Administration (SBA). www.sba.gov

- Weiss, Alan, *Million Dollar Consulting Million Dollar Consulting: The Professional's Guide to Growing a Practice,* Fifth Edition, McGraw-Hill, 2016.

- Downloads for this book may be found at www.SmallBizQuickstart.com.

Please also take a look at . . .

The Absolutely Unbreakable Rules of Service Delivery
How to Manage Your Business to Maximize Customer Service, Profit, and Employee Culture
by Karl W. Palachuk

Based on more than two decades of running successful businesses, Karl spells out the most important rules that have guided him through the years.

Whether you're staring your first business or still improving the one you have, these rules will help you to maintain profitability in any market while building a customer base that loves you and a company culture that will survive any challenge.

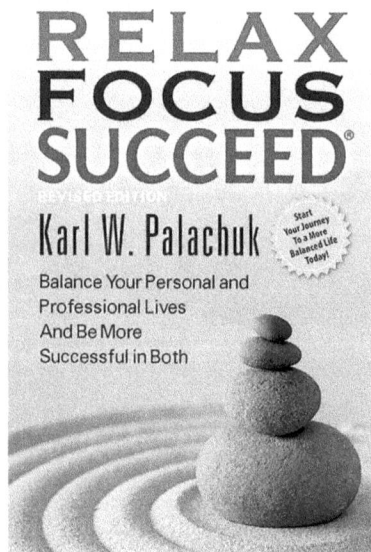

Relax Focus Succeed
Balance Your Personal and Professional Lives and Be More Successful in Both
by Karl W. Palachuk

The premise of this book is simple but powerful: The fundamental keys to success are focus, hard work, and balance. Too often, the advice we receive gives plenty of attention to focus and hard work, but very little to balance.

This great little book will help you believe that you need balance, show you the power of focus, and help you move forward with the new you — a happier, healthier, better balanced, and more successful you.